Joseph Louis La Grange

Lectures on elementary Mathematics

Joseph Louis La Grange

Lectures on elementary Mathematics

ISBN/EAN: 9783743344228

Manufactured in Europe, USA, Canada, Australia, Japa

Cover: Foto ©Paul-Georg Meister /pixelio.de

Manufactured and distributed by brebook publishing software (www.brebook.com)

Joseph Louis La Grange

Lectures on elementary Mathematics

ON ELEMENTARY MATHEMATICS

IN THE SAME SERIES.

ON CONTINUITY AND IRRATIONAL NUMBERS, and ON THE NATURE AND MEANING OF NUMBERS. By R. DEDEKIND. From the German by *W. W. Beman.* Pages, 115. Cloth, 75 cents net (3s. 6d. net).

GEOMETRIC EXERCISES IN PAPER-FOLDING. By T. SUNDARA Row. Edited and revised by *W. W. Beman* and *D. E. Smith.* With many half-tone engravings from photographs of actual exercises, and a package of papers for folding. Pages, circa 200. Cloth, $1.00. net (4s. 6d. net). (In Preparation.)

ON THE STUDY AND DIFFICULTIES OF MATHEMATICS. By AUGUSTUS DE MORGAN. Reprint edition with portrait and bibliographies. Pp., 288. Cloth, $1.25 net (4s. 6d. net).

LECTURES ON ELEMENTARY MATHEMATICS. By JOSEPH LOUIS LAGRANGE. From the French by *Thomas J. McCormack.* With portrait and biography. Pages, 172. Cloth, $1.00 net (4s. 6d. net).

ELEMENTARY ILLUSTRATIONS OF THE DIFFERENTIAL AND INTEGRAL CALCULUS. By AUGUSTUS DE MORGAN. Reprint edition. With a bibliography of textbooks of the Calculus. Pp., 144. Price, $1.00 net (4s. 6d. net).

MATHEMATICAL ESSAYS AND RECREATIONS. By PROF. HERMANN SCHUBERT, of Hamburg, Germany. From the German by *T. J. McCormack.* Essays on Number. The Magic Square, The Fourth Dimension, The Squaring of the Circle. Pages, 149. Price, Cloth. 75c. net (3s. net).

A BRIEF HISTORY OF ELEMENTARY MATHEMATICS. By DR. KARL FINK, of Tübingen. From the German by *W. W. Beman* and *D. E. Smith.* Pp. 333. Cloth, $1.50 net (5s. 6d. net).

THE OPEN COURT PUBLISHING COMPANY
324 DEARBORN ST., CHICAGO.
LONDON: Kegan Paul, Trench, Trübner & Co.

LECTURES

ON

ELEMENTARY MATHEMATICS

BY

JOSEPH LOUIS LAGRANGE

FROM THE FRENCH BY

THOMAS J. McCORMACK

SECOND EDITION

CHICAGO
THE OPEN COURT PUBLISHING COMPANY
LONDON AGENTS
KEGAN PAUL, TRENCH, TRÜBNER & Co., LTD.
1901

JAN 1907

TRANSLATION COPYRIGHTED
BY
THE OPEN COURT PUBLISHING CO.
1898.

PREFACE.

THE present work, which is a translation of the *Leçons élémentaires sur les mathematiques* of Joseph Louis Lagrange, the greatest of modern analysts, and which is to be found in Volume VII. of the new edition of his collected works, consists of a series of lectures delivered in the year 1795 at the *Ecole Normale*, —an institution which was the direct outcome of the French Revolution and which gave the first impulse to modern practical ideals of education. With Lagrange, at this institution, were associated, as professors of mathematics, Monge and Laplace, and we owe to the same historical event the final form of the famous *Géométrie descriptive*, as well as a second course of lectures on arithmetic and algebra, introductory to these of Lagrange, by Laplace.

With the exception of a German translation by Niedermüller (Leipsic, 1880), the lectures of Lagrange have never been published in separate form; originally they appeared in a fragmentary shape in the *Séances des Ecoles Normales*, as they had been reported by the stenographers, and were subsequently reprinted in the journal of the Polytechnic School. From references in them to subjects afterwards to be treated it is to be inferred that a fuller development of higher algebra was intended,—an intention which the brief existence of the *Ecole Normale* defeated. With very few exceptions, we have left the expositions in their historical form, having only referred in an Appendix to a point in the early history of algebra.

The originality, elegance, and symmetrical character of these lectures have been pointed out by DeMorgan, and notably by Dühring, who places them in the front rank of elementary expositions, as an exemplar of their kind. Coming, as they do, from one of the greatest mathematicians of modern times, and with all the excellencies which such a source implies, unique in their character as a *reading-book* in mathematics, and interwoven with historical and philosophical remarks of great helpfulness, they cannot fail to have a beneficent and stimulating influence,

The thanks of the translator of the present volume are due to Professor Henry B. Fine, of Princeton, N. J., for having read the proofs.

THOMAS J. McCORMACK.

LA SALLE, ILLINOIS, August 1, 1898.

JOSEPH LOUIS LAGRANGE.

BIOGRAPHICAL SKETCH.

A GREAT part of the progress of formal thought, where it is not hampered by outward causes, has been due to the invention of what we may call *stenophrenic*, or *short-mind*, symbols. These, of which all written language and scientific notations are examples, disengage the mind from the consideration of ponderous and circuitous mechanical operations and economise its energies for the performance of new and unaccomplished tasks of thought. And the advancement of those sciences has been most notable which have made the most extensive use of these short-mind symbols. Here mathematics and chemistry stand pre-eminent. The ancient Greeks, with all their mathematical endowment as a race, and even admitting that their powers were more visualistic than analytic, were yet so impeded by their lack of short-mind symbols as to have made scarcely any progress whatever in analysis. Their arithmetic was a species of geometry. They did not possess the sign for zero, and also did not make use of position as an indicator of value. Even later, when the germs of the indeterminate analysis were disseminated in Europe by Diophantus, progress ceased here in the science, doubtless from this very cause. The historical calculations of Archimedes, his approximation to the value of π, etc., owing to this lack of appropriate arithmetical and algebraical symbols, entailed enormous and incredible labors, which, if they had been avoided, would, with his genius, indubitably have led to great discoveries.

Subsequently, at the close of the Middle Ages, when the so-called Arabic figures became established throughout Europe with the symbol 0 and the principle of local value, immediate progress was made in the art of reckoning. The problems which arose gave rise to questions of increasing complexity and led up to the general solutions of equations of the third and fourth degree by the Italian mathematicians of the sixteenth century. Yet even these discoveries were made in somewhat the same manner as problems in mental arithmetic are now solved in common schools; for the present signs of plus, minus, and equality, the radical and exponential signs, and especially the systematic use of letters for denoting general quantities in algebra, had not yet become universal. The last step was definitively due to the French mathematician Vieta (1540–1603), and the mighty advancement of analysis resulting therefrom can hardly be measured or imagined. The trammels were here removed from algebraic thought, and it ever afterwards pursued its way unincumbered in development as if impelled by some intrinsic and irresistible potency. Then followed the introduction of exponents by Descartes, the representation of geometrical magnitudes by algebraical symbols, the extension of the theory of exponents to fractional and negative numbers by Wallis (1616–1703), and other symbolic artifices, which rendered the language of analysis as economic, unequivocal, and appropriate as the needs of the science appeared to demand. In the famous dispute regarding the invention of the infinitesimal calculus, while not denying and even granting for the nonce the priority of Newton in the matter, some writers have gone so far as to regard Leibnitz's introduction of the integral symbol $\int$ as alone a sufficient substantiation of his claims to originality and independence, so far as the power of the new science was concerned.

For the *development* of science all such short-mind symbols are of paramount importance, and seem to carry within themselves the germ of a perpetual mental motion which needs no outward power for its unfoldment. Euler's well-known saying that his pencil seemed to surpass him in intelligence finds its explanation here, and will be understood by all who have experienced the uncanny feeling attending the rapid development of algebraical formulæ, where the urned thought of centuries, so to speak, rolls from one's finger's ends.

But it should never be forgotten that the mighty stenophrenic engine of which we here speak, like all machinery, affords us rather a mastery over nature than an insight into it; and for some, unfortunately, the higher symbols of mathematics are merely brambles that hide the living springs of reality. Many of the greatest discoveries of science,—for example, those of Galileo, Huygens, and Newton,—were made without the mechanism which afterwards becomes so indispensable for their development and application. Galileo's reasoning anent the summation of the impulses imparted to a falling stone is virtual integration; and Newton's mechanical discoveries were made by the man who invented, but evidently did not use to that end, the doctrine of fluxions.

* * *

We have been following here, briefly and roughly, a line of progressive abstraction and generalisation which even in its beginning was, psychologically speaking, at an exalted height, but in the course of centuries had been carried to points of literally ethereal refinement and altitude. In that long succession of inquirers by whom this result was effected, the process reached, we may say, its culmination and purest expression in Joseph Louis Lagrange, born in Turin, Italy, the 30th of January, 1736, died in Paris, April 10, 1813. Lagrange's power over symbols has, perhaps, never been paralleled either before his day or since. It is amusing to hear his biographers relate that in early life he evinced no aptitude for mathematics, but seemed to have been given over entirely to the pursuits of pure literature; for at fifteen we find him teaching mathematics in an artillery school in Turin, and at nineteen he had made the greatest discovery in mathematical science since that of the infinitesimal calculus, namely, the creation of the algorism and method of the Calculus of Variations. "Your analytical solution of the isoperimetrical problem," writes Euler, then the prince of European mathematicians, to him, "leaves nothing to be desired in this department of inquiry, and I am delighted beyond measure that it has been your lot to carry to the highest pitch of perfection, a theory, which since its inception I have been almost the only one to cultivate." But the exact nature of a "variation" even Euler did not grasp, and even as late as 1810 in the English treatise of Woodhouse on this subject we read regarding a certain new sign introduced, that M. Lagrange's "power over symbols is so unbounded that the possession of it seems to have made him capricious."

Lagrange himself was conscious of his wonderful capacities in this direction. His was a time when geometry, as he himself phrased it, had become a dead language, the abstractions of analysis were being pushed to their highest pitch, and he felt that with his achievements its possibilities within certain limits were being rapidly exhausted. The saying is attributed to him that chairs of mathematics, so far as creation was concerned, and unless new fields were opened up, would soon be as rare at universities as chairs of Arabic. In both research and exposition, he totally reversed the methods of his predecessors. They had proceeded in their exposition from special cases by a species of induction; his eye was always directed to the highest and most general points of view; and it was by his suppression of details and neglect of minor, unimportant considerations that he swept the whole field of analysis with a generality of insight and power never excelled, adding to his originality and profundity a conciseness, elegance, and lucidity which have made him the model of mathematical writers.

* * *

Lagrange came of an old French family of Touraine, France, said to have been allied to that of Descartes. At the age of twenty-six he found himself at the zenith of European fame. But his reputation had been purchased at a great cost. Although of ordinary height and well proportioned, he had by his ecstatic devotion to study,—periods always accompanied by an irregular pulse and high febrile excitatian,—almost ruined his health. At this age, accordingly, he was seized with a hypochondriacal affection and with bilious disorders, which accompanied him thronghout his life, and which were only allayed by his great abstemiousness and careful regimen. He was bled twenty-nine times, an infliction which alone would have affected the most robust constitution. Through his great care for his health he gave much attention to medicine. He was, in fact, conversant with all the sciences, although knowing his *forte* he rarely expressed an opinion on anything unconnected with mathematics.

When Euler left Berlin for St. Petersburg in 1766 he and D'Alembert induced Frederick the Great to make Lagrange president of the Academy of Sciences at Berlin. Lagrange accepted the position and lived in Berlin twenty years, where he wrote some of his greatest works. He was a great favorite of the Berlin people, and enjoyed the profoundest respect of Frederick the Great, although the latter seems to have preferred the noisy reputation of Maupertuis, Lamettrie, and Voltaire to the unobtrusive fame and personality of the man whose achievements were destined to shed more lasting light on his reign than those of any of his more strident literary predecessors : Lagrange was, as he himself said, *philosophe sans crier*.

The climate of Prussia agreed with the mathematician. He refused the most seductive offers of foreign courts and princes, and it was not until the death of Frederick and the intellectual reaction of the Prussian court that he returned to Paris, where his career broke forth in renewed splendor. He published in 1788 his great *Mécanique analytique*, that "scientific poem" of Sir William Rowan Hamilton, which gave the quietus to mechanics as then formulated, and having been made during the Revolution Professor of Mathematics at the new *Ecole Normale* and the *Ecole Polytechnique*, he entered with Laplace and Monge upon the activity which made these schools for generations to come exemplars of practical scientific education, systematising by his lectures there, and putting into definitive form, the science of mathematical analysis of which he had developed the extremest capacities. Lagrange's activity at Paris was interrupted only once by a brief period of melancholy aversion for mathematics, a lull which he devoted to the adolescent science of chemistry and to philosophical studies; but he afterwards resumed his old love with increased ardor and assiduity. His significance for thought generally is far beyond what we have space to insist upon. Not least of all, theology, which had invariably mingled itself with the researches of his predecessors, was with him forever divorced from a legitimate influence of science.

The honors of the world sat ill upon Lagrange: *la magnificence le gênait*, he said; but he lived at a time when proffered things were usually accepted, not refused. He was loaded with personal favors and official distinctions by Napoleon who called him *la haute pyramide des sciences mathématiques*, was made a Senator, a Count of the Empire, a Grand Officer of the Legion of Honor, and, just before his death, received the grand cross of the Order of Reunion. He never feared death, which he termed *une dernière fonction, ni pénible ni désagréable*, much less the disapproval of the great. He remained in Paris during the Revolution when *savants* were decidedly in disfavor, but was suspected of aspiring to no throne but that of mathematics. When Lavoisier was executed he said: "It took them but a moment to lay low that head; yet a hundred years will not suffice perhaps to produce its like again."

Lagrange would never allow his portrait to be painted, maintaining that a man's works and not his personality deserved preservation. The frontispiece to the present work is from a steel engraving based on a sketch obtained by stealth at a meeting of the Institute. His genius was excelled only by the purity and nobleness of his character, in which the world never even sought to find a blot, and by the exalted Pythagorean simplicity of his life. He was twice married, and by his wonderful care of his person lived to the advanced age of seventy-seven years, not one of which had been misspent. His life was the veriest incarnation of the scientific spirit; he lived for nothing else. He left his weak body, which retained its intellectual powers to the very last, as an offering upon the altar of science, happily made when his work had been done; but to the world he bequeathed his "ever-living" thoughts now recently resurgent in a new and monumental edition of his works (published by Gauthier-Villars, Paris). *Ma vie est là!* he said, pointing to his brain the day before his death.

THOMAS J. MCCORMACK.

CONTENTS.

	PAGES
PREFACE	
BIOGRAPHICAL SKETCH OF JOSEPH LOUIS LAGRANGE.	

LECTURE I. ON ARITHMETIC, AND IN PARTICULAR FRACTIONS AND LOGARITHMS. 1–23
Systems of Numeration.—Fractions.—Greatest Common Divisor.—Continued Fractions.—Theory of Powers, Proportions, and Progressions.—Involution and Evolution.—Rule of Three.—Interest.—Annuities.—Logarithms.

LECTURE II. ON THE OPERATIONS OF ARITHMETIC . . . 24–53
Arithmetic and Geometry.—New Method of Subtraction.—Abridged and Approximate Multiplication.—Decimals.—Property of the Number 9.—Tests of Divisibility.—Theory of Remainders.—Checks on Multiplication and Division.—Evolution.—Rule of Three.—Theory and Practice.—Probability of Life.—Alligation or the Rule of Mixtures.

LECTURE III. ON ALGEBRA, PARTICULARLY THE RESOLUTION OF EQUATIONS OF THE THIRD AND FOURTH DEGREE 54–95
Origin of Greek Algebra.—Diophantus.—Indeterminate Analysis.—Equations of the Second Degree.—Translations of Diophantus.—Algebra Among the Arabs.—History of Algebra in Italy, France, and Germany.—History of Equations of the Third and Fourth Degree and of the Irreducible Case.—Theory of Equations.—Discussion of Cubic Equations.—Discussion of the Irreducible Case.—The Theory

CONTENTS.

PAGES

of Roots.—Extraction of the Square and Cube Roots of Two Imaginary Binomials.—Theory of Imaginary Expressions.—Trisection of an Angle.—Method of Indeterminates.—Discussion of Biquadratic Equations.

LECTURE IV. ON THE RESOLUTION OF NUMERICAL EQUATIONS 96–126
Algebraical Resolution of Equations.—Numerical Resolution of Equations.—Position of the Roots.—Representation of Equations by Curves.—Graphic Resolution of Equations.—Character of the Roots of Equations.—Limits of the Roots of Numerical Equations.—Separation of the Roots.—Method of Substitutions.—The Equation of Differences.—Method of Elimination.—Constructions and Instruments for Solving Equations.

LECTURE V. ON THE EMPLOYMENT OF CURVES IN THE SOLUTION OF PROBLEMS. 127–149
Application of Geometry to Algebra.—Resolution of Problems by Curves.—The Problem of Two Lights.—Variable Quantities.—Minimal Values.—Analysis of Biquadratic Equations Conformably to the Problem of the Two Lights.—Advantages of the Method of Curves —The Curve of Errors.—*Regula falsi.*—Solution of Problems by the Curve of Errors.—Problem of the Circle and Inscribed Polygon.—Problem of the Observer and Three Objects.—Parabolic Curves.—Newton's Problem.—Interpolation of Intermediate Terms in Series of Observations, Experiments, etc.

APPENDIX 151
Note on the Origin of Algebra.

LECTURE I.

ON ARITHMETIC, AND IN PARTICULAR FRACTIONS AND LOGARITHMS.

ARITHMETIC is divided into two parts. The first is based on the decimal system of notation and on the manner of arranging numeral characters to express numbers. This first part comprises the four common operations of addition, subtraction, multiplication, and division,—operations which, as you know, would be different if a different system were adopted, but, which it would not be difficult to transform from one system to another, if a change of systems were desirable. *Systems of numeration*

The second part is independent of the system of numeration. It is based on the consideration of quantities and on the general properties of numbers. The theory of fractions, the theory of powers and of roots, the theory of arithmetical and geometrical progressions, and, lastly, the theory of logarithms, fall under this head. I purpose to advance, here, some remarks on the different branches of this part of arithmetic.

It may be regarded as *universal arithmetic*, having an intimate affinity to algebra. For, if instead of particularising the quantities considered, if instead of assigning them numerically, we treat them in quite a general way, designating them by letters, we have algebra.

Fractions. You know what a fraction is. The notion of a fraction is slightly more composite than that of whole numbers. In whole numbers we consider simply a quantity repeated. To reach the notion of a fraction it is necessary to consider the quantity divided into a certain number of parts. Fractions represent in general ratios, and serve to express one quantity by means of another. In general, nothing measurable can be measured except by fractions expressing the result of the measurement, unless the measure be contained an exact number of times in the thing to be measured.

You also know how a fraction can be reduced to its lowest terms. When the numerator and the denominator are both divisible by the same number, their greatest common divisor can be found by a very ingenious method which we owe to Euclid. This method is exceedingly simple and lucid, but it may be rendered even more palpable to the eye by the following consideration. Suppose, for example, that you have a given length, and that you wish to measure it. The unit of measure is given, and you wish to know how many times it is contained in the length. You first lay off your measure as many times as you can on the given length, and that gives you a certain whole number of measures. If there is no remainder your operation is finished. But if there be a remainder, that remainder is still to be evaluated. If the measure is divided into equal parts, for example, into ten, twelve, or more equal parts, the natural procedure is to use one of these parts as a new measure and to see how many times it is contained in the remainder. You will then have for the value of your remainder, a fraction of which the numerator is the number of parts contained in the remainder and the denominator the total number of parts into which the given measure is divided. *Greatest common divisor.*

I will suppose, now, that your measure is not so divided but that you still wish to determine the ratio of the proposed length to the length which you have adopted as your measure. The following is the procedure which most naturally suggests itself.

If you have a remainder, since that is less than the measure, naturally you will seek to find how many times your remainder is contained in this measure. Let us say two times, and that a remainder is still left. Lay this remainder on the preceding remainder. Since it is necessarily smaller, it will still be contained a certain number of times in the preceding remainder, say three times, and there will be another remainder or there will not ; and so on. In these different remainders you will have what is called a *continued fraction*. For example, you have found that the measure is contained three times in the proposed length. You have, to start with, the number *three*. Then you have found that your first remainder is contained twice in your measure. You will have the fraction *one* divided by *two*. But this last denominator is not complete, for it was supposed there was still a remainder. That remainder will give another and similar fraction, which is to be added to the last denominator, and which by our supposition is *one* divided by *three*. And so with the rest. You will then have the fraction

<small>Continued fractions.</small>

$$3+\cfrac{1}{2+\cfrac{1}{3+\cdots}}$$

as the expression of your ratio between the proposed length and the adopted measure.

Fractions of this form are called *continued fractions*, and can be reduced to ordinary fractions by the common rules. Thus, if we stop at the first fraction, i. e., if we consider only the first remainder and neglect the second, we shall have $3+\frac{1}{2}$, which is equal to $\frac{7}{2}$. Considering only the first and the second remainders, we stop at the second fraction, and shall have $3+\cfrac{1}{2+\frac{1}{3}}$. Now $2+\frac{1}{3}=\frac{7}{3}$. We shall have therefore $3+\frac{3}{7}$, which is equal to $\frac{24}{7}$. And so on with the rest. If we arrive in the course of the operation at a remainder which is contained exactly in the preceding remainder, the operation is terminated, and we shall have in the continued fraction a common fraction that is the exact value of the length to be measured, in terms of the length which served as our measure. If the operation is not thus terminated, it can be continued to infinity, and we shall have only fractions which approach more and more nearly to the true value.

Terminating continued fractions.

If we now compare this procedure with that employed for finding the greatest common divisor of two numbers, we shall see that it is virtually the same thing; the difference being that in finding the greatest common divisor we devote our attention solely to the different remainders, of which the last is the divisor sought, whereas by employing the successive quotients, as we have done above, we obtain fractions which constantly approach nearer and nearer to the fraction formed by the two numbers given, and of which the last is that fraction itself reduced to its lowest terms.

As the theory of continued fractions is little known, but is yet of great utility in the solution of important numerical questions, I shall enter here somewhat more fully into the formation and properties of these fractions. And, first, let us suppose that the quotients found, whether by the mechanical operation, or by the method for finding the greatest common divisor, are, as above, 3, 2, 3, 5, 7, 3. The following is a rule by which we can write down at once the convergent fractions which result from these quotients, without developing the continued fraction.

The first quotient, supposed divided by unity, will give the first fraction, which will be too small, Converging namely, $\frac{3}{1}$. Then, multiplying the numerator and denominator of this fraction by the second quotient and adding unity to the numerator, we shall have the second fraction, $\frac{7}{2}$, which will be too large. Multiplying in like manner the numerator and denominator of this fraction by the third quotient, and adding to the numerator the numerator of the preceding fraction, and to the denominator the denominator of the preceding fraction, we shall have the third fraction, which will be too small. Thus, the third quotient being 3, we have for our numerator $(7 \times 3 = 21) + 3 = 24$, and for our denominator $(2 \times 3 = 6) + 1 = 7$. The third convergent, therefore, is $\frac{24}{7}$. We proceed in the same manner for the fourth convergent. The fourth quotient being 5, we say 24 times 5 is 120, and this plus 7, the numerator of the fraction preceding, is 127; similarly, 7 times 5 is 35, and this plus 2 is 37. The new fraction, therefore, is $\frac{127}{37}$. And so with the rest.

In this manner, by employing the six quotients 3, 2, 3, 5, 7, 3 we obtain the six fractions

$$\frac{3}{1}, \frac{7}{2}, \frac{24}{7}, \frac{127}{37}, \frac{913}{266}, \frac{2866}{835},$$

of which the last, supposing the operation to be completed at the sixth quotient 3, will be the required value of the length measured, or the fraction itself reduced to its lowest terms.

The fractions which precede the last are alternately

smaller and larger than the last, and have the advantage of approaching more and more nearly to its value in such wise that no other fraction can approach it more nearly except its denominator be larger than the product of the denominator of the fraction in question and the denominator of the fraction following. For example, the fraction $\frac{24}{7}$ is less than the true value which is that of the fraction $\frac{2866}{835}$, but it approaches to it more nearly than any other fraction does whose denominator is not greater than the product of 7 by 37, that is, 259. Thus, any fraction expressed in large numbers may be reduced to a series of fractions expressed in smaller numbers and which approach as near to it as possible in value.

Convergents.

The demonstration of the foregoing properties is deduced from the nature of continued fractions, and from the fact that if we seek the difference between one of the convergent fractions and that next adjacent to it we shall obtain a fraction of which the numerator is always unity and the denominator the product of the two denominators; a consequence which follows *a priori* from the very law of formation of these fractions. Thus the difference between $\frac{7}{2}$ and $\frac{3}{4}$ is $\frac{1}{2}$, in excess; between $\frac{24}{7}$ and $\frac{7}{2}$, $\frac{1}{14}$, in defect; between $\frac{127}{37}$ and $\frac{24}{7}$, $\frac{1}{259}$, in excess; and so on. The result being, that by employing this series of differences we can express in another and very simple manner the fractions with which we are here concerned, by means of a second series of fractions of which the numerators are all unity and the denominators successively the products of every two adjacent denominators. Instead of the fractions written above, we have thus the series:

A second method of expression.

$$\frac{3}{1} + \frac{1}{1\times 2} - \frac{1}{2\times 7} + \frac{1}{7\times 37} - \frac{1}{37\times 266} + \frac{1}{266\times 835}.$$

The first term, as we see, is the first fraction, the first and second together give the second fraction $\frac{7}{2}$, the first, the second, and the third give the third fraction $\frac{24}{7}$, and so on with the rest; the result being that the series entire is equivalent to the last fraction.

There is still another way, less known but in some respects more simple, of treating the same question—which leads directly to a series similar to the preceding. Reverting to the previous example, after having found that the measure goes three times into the length to be measured and that after the first remainder has been applied to the measure there is left a new remainder, instead of comparing this second remainder with the preceding, as we did above, we may compare it with the measure itself. Thus, supposing it goes into the latter seven times with a remainder, we again compare this last remainder with the measure, and so on, until we arrive, if possible, at a remainder which is an aliquot part of the measure,—which will terminate the operation. In the contrary event, if the measure and the length to be measured are incommensurable, the process may be continued to infinity.

We shall have then, as the expression of the length measured, the series

$$3 + \frac{1}{2} - \frac{1}{2 \times 7} + \ldots \ldots$$

A third method of expression.

It is clear that this method is also applicable to ordinary fractions. We constantly retain the denominator of the fraction as the dividend, and take the different remainders successively as divisors. Thus, the fraction $\frac{2800}{835}$ gives the quotients 3, 2, 7, 18, 19, 46, 119, 417 835; from which we obtain the series

$$3 + \frac{1}{2} - \frac{1}{2 \times 7} + \frac{1}{2 \times 7 \times 18} - \frac{1}{2 \times 7 \times 18 \times 19} + \ldots ;$$

and as these partial fractions rapidly diminish, we shall have, by combining them successively, the simple fractions,

$$\frac{7}{2}, \quad \frac{48}{2 \times 7}, \quad \frac{865}{2 \times 7 \times 18}, \quad \ldots ,$$

which will constantly approach nearer and nearer to the true value sought, and the error will be less than the first of the partial fractions neglected.

Our remarks on the foregoing methods of evaluating fractions should not be construed as signifying that the employment of decimal fractions is not nearly always preferable for expressing the values of fractions to whatever degree of exactness we wish. But cases occur where it is necessary that these values should be expressed by as few figures as possible. For example, if it were required to construct a planetarium, since the ratios of the revolutions of the planets to one another are expressed by very large numbers, it would be necessary, in order not to multiply unduly the number of the teeth on the wheels, to avail ourselves of smaller numbers, but at the same time so to select them that their ratios should approach as nearly as possible to the actual ratios. It was, in fact, this very question that prompted Huygens, in his search for its solution, to resort to continued fractions and that so gave birth to the theory of these fractions. Afterwards, in the elaboration of this theory, it was found adapted to the solution of other important questions, and this is the reason, since it is not found in elementary works, that I have deemed it necessary to go somewhat into detail in expounding its principles.

Origin of continued fractions.

We will now pass to the theory of powers, proportions, and progressions.

As you already know, a number multiplied by itself gives its square, and multiplied again by itself gives its cube, and so on. In geometry we do not go beyond the cube, because no body can have more than three dimensions. But in algebra and arithmetic we may go as far as we please. And here the theory of the extraction of roots takes its origin. For, although every number can be raised to its square and to its cube and so forth, it is not true reciprocally that every number is an exact square or an exact cube. The number 2, for example, is not a square; for the square of 1 is 1, and the square of 2 is four; and there being no other whole numbers between these two, it is impossible to find a whole number which multiplied by itself will give 2. It cannot be found in fractions, for if you take a fraction reduced to its lowest terms, the square of that fraction will again be a fraction reduced to its lowest terms, and consequently cannot be equal to the whole number 2. But though we cannot obtain the square root of 2 exactly, we can yet approach to it as nearly as we please, particularly by decimal fractions. By following the common rules for the extraction of square roots, cube roots, and so forth, the process may be extended to infinity, and the true values of the roots may be approximated to any degree of exactitude we wish.

Involution and evolution.

But I shall not enter into details here. The theory of powers has given rise to that of progressions, before entering on which a word is necessary on proportions.

Every fraction expresses a ratio. Having two equal fractions, therefore, we have two equal ratios; and the numbers constituting the fractions or the ratios form what is called a *proportion*. Thus the equality of the ratios 2 to 4 and 3 to 6 gives the proportion $2:4::3:6$, because 4 is the double of 2 as 6 is the double of 3. Many of the rules of arithmetic depend on the theory of proportions. First, it is the foundation of the famous *rule of three*, which is so extensively used. You know that when the first three terms of a proportion are given, to obtain the fourth you have only to multiply the last two together and divide the product by the first. Various special rules have also been conceived and have found a place in the books on arithmetic; but they are all reducible to the rule of three and may be neglected if we once thoroughly grasp the conditions of the problem. There are direct, inverse, simple, and compound rules of three, rules of partnership, of mixtures, and so forth. In all cases it is only necessary to consider carefully the conditions of the problem and to arrange the terms of the proportion correspondingly.

<small>Proportions</small>

I shall not enter into further details here. There is, however, another theory which is useful on numerous occasions,—namely, the *theory of progressions*. When you have several numbers that bear the same proportion to one another, and which follow one another in such a manner that the second is to the first as the third is to the second, as the fourth is to the third, and so forth, these numbers form a progression. I shall begin with an observation.

The books of arithmetic and algebra ordinarily distinguish between two kinds of progression, arithmetical and geometrical, corresponding to the proportions called arithmetical and geometrical. But the appellation proportion appears to me extremely inappropriate as applied to *arithmetical proportion*. And as it is one of the objects of the *École Normale* to rectify the language of science, the present slight digression will not be considered irrelevant.

I take it, then, that the idea of proportion is already well established by usage and that it corresponds solely to what is called *geometrical proportion*. When we speak of the proportion of the parts of a man's body, of the proportion of the parts of an edifice, etc.; when we say that a plan should be reduced proportionately in size, etc.; in fact, when we say generally that one thing is proportional to another, we understand by proportion equality of ratios only, as in geometrical proportion, and never equality of differences as in arithmetical proportion. Therefore, instead of saying that the numbers, 3, 5, 7, 9, are in arithmetical proportion, because the difference between 5 and 3 is the same as that between 9 and 7, I deem it desirable that some other term should be employed, so as to avoid all ambiguity. We might, for instance, call such numbers *equi-different*, reserving the name of *proportionals* for numbers that are in geometrical proportion, as 2, 4, 6, 8, etc.

As for the rest, I cannot see why the proportion called *arithmetical* is any more arithmetical than that which is called geometrical, nor why the latter is more geometrical than the former. On the contrary, the primitive idea of geometrical proportion is based on arithmetic, for the notion of ratios springs essentially from the consideration of numbers.

Still, in waiting for these inappropriate designations to be changed, I shall continue to make use of them, as a matter of simplicity and convenience.

[margin: Arithmetical and geometrical proportions.]

Progressions.

The theory of arithmetical progressions presents few difficulties. Arithmetical progressions consist of quantities which increase or diminish constantly by the same amount. But the theory of geometrical progressions is more difficult and more important, as a large number of interesting questions depend upon it —for example, all problems of compound interest, all problems that relate to discount, and many others of like nature.

In general, quantities in geometrical proportion are produced, when a quantity increases and the force generating the increase, so to speak, is proportional to that quantity. It has been observed that in countries where the means of subsistence are easy of acquisition, as in the first American colonies, the population is doubled at the expiration of twenty years; if it is doubled at the end of twenty years it will be quadrupled at the end of forty, octupled at the end of sixty, and so on; the result being, as we see, a geometrical progression, corresponding to intervals of time in arithmetical progression. It is the same with compound interest. If a given sum of money produces, at the expiration of a certain time, a certain sum, at the end of double that time, the original sum will have produced an equivalent additional sum, and in addition the sum produced in the first space of time will, in its proportion, likewise have produced during the second space of time a certain sum; and so with the rest. The original sum is commonly called the *prin-*

cipal, the sum produced the *interest*, and the constant ratio of the principal to the interest per annum, the *rate*. Thus, the rate *twenty* signifies that the interest is the twentieth part of the principal,—a rate which is commonly called 5 *per cent.*, 5 being the twentieth part of 100. On this basis, the principal, at the end of one year, will have increased by its one-twentieth part; consequently, it will have been augmented in the ratio of 21 to 20. At the end of two years, it will have been increased again in the same ratio, that is in the ratio of $\frac{21}{20}$ multiplied by $\frac{21}{20}$; at the end of three years, in the ratio of $\frac{21}{20}$ multiplied twice by itself; and so on. In this manner we shall find that at the end of fifteen years it will almost have doubled itself, and that at the end of fifty-three years it will have increased tenfold. Conversely, then, since a sum paid now will be doubled at the end of fifteen years, it is clear that a sum not payable till after the expiration of fifteen years is now worth only one-half its amount. This is what is termed the *present value* of a sum payable at the end of a certain time; and it is plain, that to find that value, it is only necessary to divide the sum promised by the fraction $\frac{21}{20}$, or to multiply it by the fraction $\frac{20}{21}$, as many times as there are years for the sum to run. In this way we shall find that a sum payable at the end of fifty-three years, is worth at present only one-tenth. From this it is evident what little advantage is to be derived from surrendering the absolute ownership of a sum of money in order to ob-

Compound interest.

tain the enjoyment of it for a period of only fifty years, say; seeing that we gain by such a transaction only one-tenth in actual use, whilst we lose the ownership of the property forever.

<small>Present values and annuities.</small>

In *annuities*, the consideration of interest is combined with that of the probability of life; and as every one is prone to believe that he will live very long, and as, on the other hand, one is apt to underestimate the value of property which must be abandoned on death, a peculiar temptation arises, when one is without children, to invest one's fortune, wholly or in part, in annuities. Nevertheless, when put to the test of rigorous calculation, annuities are not found to offer sufficient advantages to induce people to sacrifice for them the ownership of the original capital. Accordingly, whenever it has been attempted to create annuities sufficiently attractive to induce individuals to invest in them, it has been necessary to offer them on terms which are onerous to the company.

But we shall have more to say on this subject when we expound the theory of annuities, which is a branch of the calculus of probabilities.

I shall conclude the present lecture with a word on *logarithms*. The simplest idea which we can form of the theory of logarithms, as they are found in the ordinary tables, is that of conceiving all numbers as powers of 10; the exponents of these powers, then, will be the logarithms of the numbers. From this it is evident that the multiplication and division of two numbers is reducible to the addition and subtraction of their respective exponents, that is, of their logarithms. And, consequently, involution and the extraction of roots are reducible to multiplication and division, which is of immense advantage in arithmetic and renders logarithms of priceless value in that science. Logarithms

But in the period when logarithms were invented, mathematicians were not in possession of the theory of powers. They did not know that the root of a number could be represented by a fractional power. The following was the way in which they approached the problem.

The primitive idea was that of two corresponding progressions, one arithmetical, and the other geometrical. In this way the general notion of a logarithm was reached. But the means for finding the logarithms of all numbers were still lacking. As the numbers follow one another in arithmetical progression, it was requisite, in order that they might all be found among the terms of a geometrical progression, so to establish that progression that its successive terms should differ by extremely small quantities from one another; and, to prove the possibility of expressing all numbers in this way, Napier, the inventor, first considered them as expressed by lines and parts of lines, and these lines he considered as generated by the continuous motion of a point, which was quite natural.

Napier (1550–1617).

He considered, accordingly, two lines, the first of which was generated by the motion of a point describing in equal times spaces in geometrical progression, and the other generated by a point which described spaces that increased as the times and consequently formed an arithmetical progression corresponding to the geometrical progression. And he supposed, for the sake of simplicity, that the initial velocities of these two points were equal. This gave him the logarithms, at first called *natural*, and afterwards *hyperbolical*, when it was discovered that they could be expressed as parts of the area included between a hyperbola and its asymptotes. By this method it is clear that to find the logarithm of any given number, it is only necessary to take a part on the first line equal to the given number, and to seek the part on the second line which shall have been described in the same interval of time as the part on the first.

Conformably to this idea, if we take as the two first terms of our geometrical progression the numbers with very small differences 1 and 1.0000001, and as those of our arithmetical progression 0 and 0.0000001, and if we seek successively, by the known rules, all the following terms of the two progressions, we shall find that the number 2 expressed approximately to the eighth place of decimals is the 6931472th term of the geometrical progression, that is, that the logarithm o

2 is 0.6931472. The number 10 will be found to be the 23025851th term of the same progression; therefore, the logarithm of 10 is 2.3025851, and so with the rest. But Napier, having to determine only the logarithms of numbers less than unity for the purposes of trigonometry, where the sines and cosines of angles are expressed as fractions of the radius, considered a decreasing geometrical progression of which the first two terms were 1 and 0.9999999; and of this progression he determined the succeeding terms by enormous computations. On this last hypothesis, the logarithm which we have just found for 2 becomes that of the number $\frac{1}{2}$ or 0.5, and that of the number 10 becomes that of the number $\frac{1}{10}$ or 0.1; as is readily apparent from the nature of the two progressions.

Origin of logarithms

Napier's work appeared in 1614. Its utility was felt at once. But it was also immediately seen that it would conform better to the decimal system of our arithmetic, and would be simpler, if the logarithm of 10 were made unity, conformably to which that of 100 would be 2, and so with the rest. To that end, instead of taking as the first two terms of our geometrical progression the numbers 1 and 0.0000001, we should have to take the numbers 1 and 1.0000002302, retaining 0 and 0.0000001 as the corresponding terms of the arithmetical progression. Whence it will be seen, that, while the point which is supposed to generate by its motion the geometrical line, or the numbers, is describing the very small portion 0.0000002302 . . . , the other point, the office of which is to generate simultaneously the arithmetical line, will have described the portion 0.0000001; and that therefore the spaces described in the same time by the two points at the beginning of their motion, that is to say, their initial velocities, instead of being equal, as in the preceding system, will be in the proportion of the numbers 2.302 . . . to 1, where it will be remarked that the number 2.302 . . . is exactly the number which in the original system of natural logarithms stood for the logarithm of 10,—a result demonstrable *à priori*, as we shall see when we come to apply the formulæ of algebra to the theory of logarithms. Briggs, a contemporary of Napier, is the author of this change in the system of logarithms, as he is also of the tables of logarithms now in common use. A portion of these was calculated by Briggs himself, and the remainder by Vlacq, a Dutchman.

_{Briggs (1556-1631). Vlacq.}

These tables appeared at Gouda, in 1628. They contain the logarithms of all numbers from 1 to 100000 to ten decimal places, and are now extremely rare. But it was afterwards discovered that for ordinary purposes seven decimals were sufficient, and the logarithms are found in this form in the tables which are used to-day. Briggs and Vlacq employed a number of highly ingenious artifices for facilitating their work. The device which offered itself most naturally and which is still one of the simplest, consists in taking the numbers 1, 10, 100, . . . , of which the logarithms

ON ARITHMETIC.

are 0, 1, 2, ... , and in interpolating between the successive terms of these two series as many corresponding terms as we desire, in the first series by geometrical mean proportionals and in the second by arithmetical means. In this manner, when we have arrived at a term of the first series approaching, to the eighth decimal place, the number whose logarithm we seek, the corresponding term of the other series will be, to the eighth decimal place approximately, the logarithm of that number. Thus, to obtain the logarithm of 2, since 2 lies between 1 and 10, we seek first by the extraction of the square root of 10, the geometrical mean between 1 and 10, which we find to be 3.16227766, while the corresponding arithmetical mean between 0 and 1 is $\frac{1}{2}$ or 0.50000000; we are assured thus that this last number is the logarithm of the first. Again, as 2 lies between 1 and 3.16227766, the number just found, we seek in the same manner the geometrical mean between these two numbers, and find the number 1.77827941. As before, taking the arithmetical mean between 0 and 5.0000000, we shall have for the logarithm of 1.77827941 the number 0.25000000. Again, 2 lying between 1.77827941 and 3.16227766, it will be necessary, for still further approximation, to find the geometrical mean between these two, and likewise the arithmetical mean between their logarithms. And so on. In this manner, by a large number of similar operations, we find that the logarithm of 2 is 0.3010300, that of 3 is 0.4771213,

Computation of logarithms.

ON ARITHMETIC.

Value of the history of science.

and so on, not carrying the degree of exactness beyond the seventh decimal place. But the preceding calculation is necessary only for prime numbers; because the logarithms of numbers which are the product of two or several others, are found by simply taking the sum of the logarithms of their factors.

As for the rest, since the calculation of logarithms is now a thing of the past, except in isolated instances, it may be thought that the details into which we have here entered are devoid of value. We may, however, justly be curious to know the trying and tortuous paths which the great inventors have trodden, the different steps which they have taken to attain their goal, and the extent to which we are indebted to these veritable benefactors of the human race. Such knowledge, moreover, is not matter of idle curiosity. It can afford us guidance in similar inquiries and sheds an increased light on the subjects with which we are employed.

Logarithms are an instrument universally employed in the sciences, and in the arts depending on calculation. The following, for example, is a very evident application of their use.

Persons not entirely unacquainted with music know that the different notes of the octave are expressed by numbers which give the divisions of a stretched cord producing those notes. Thus, the principal note being denoted by 1, its octave will be denoted by $\frac{1}{2}$, its fifth by $\frac{2}{3}$, its third by $\frac{4}{5}$, its fourth by $\frac{3}{4}$, its second by $\frac{9}{8}$, and so on. The distance of one of these notes from that next adjacent to it is called an *interval*, and is measured, not by the difference, but by the ratio of the numbers expressing the two sounds. Thus, the interval between the fourth and fifth, which is called the *major tone*, is regarded as sensibly double of that between the third and fourth, which is called the *semi-major*. In fact, the first being expressed by $\frac{9}{8}$, the second by $\frac{16}{15}$, it can be easily proved that the first does not differ by much from the square of the second. Now, it is clear that this conception of intervals, on which the whole theory of temperament is founded, conducts us naturally to logarithms. For if we express the value of the different notes by the logarithms of the lengths of the cords answering to them, then the interval of one note from another will be expressed by the simple difference of values of the two notes; and if it were required to divide the octave into twelve equal semi-tones, which would give the temperament that is simplest and most exact, we should simply have to divide the logarithm of one half, the value of the octave, into twelve equal parts.

Musical temperament.

LECTURE II.

ON THE OPERATIONS OF ARITHMETIC.

<small>Arithmetic and geometry.</small>

AN ANCIENT writer once remarked that arithmetic and geometry were *the wings of mathematics*. I believe we can say, without metaphor, that these two sciences are the foundation and essence of all the sciences that treat of magnitude. But not only are they the foundation, they are also, so to speak, the capstone of these sciences. For, whenever we have reached a result, in order to make use of it, it is requisite that it be translated into numbers or into lines; to translate it into numbers, arithmetic is necessary; to translate it into lines, we must have recourse to geometry.

The importance of arithmetic, accordingly, leads me to the further discussion of that subject to-day, although we have begun algebra. I shall take up its several parts, and shall offer new observations, which will serve to supplement what I have already expounded to you. I shall employ, moreover, the geometrical calculus, wherever that is necessary for giv-

ON THE OPERATIONS OF ARITHMETIC. 25

ing greater generality to the demonstrations and methods.

First, then, as regards addition, there is nothing to be added to what has already been said. Addition is an operation so simple in character that its conception is a matter of course. But with regard to subtraction, there is another manner of performing that operation which is frequently more advantageous than the common method, particularly for those familiar with it. It consists in converting the subtraction into addition by taking the complement of every figure of the number which is to be subtracted, first with respect to 10 and afterwards with respect to 9. Suppose, for example, that the number 2635 is to be subtracted from the number 7853. Instead of saying 5 *[New method of subtraction]*

$$\begin{array}{r} 7853 \\ 2635 \\ \hline 5218 \end{array}$$

from 13 leaves 8; 3 from 4 leaves 1; 6 from 8 leaves 2; and 2 from 7 leaves 5, giving a total remainder of 5218,— I say: 5 the complement of 5 with respect to 10 added to 3 gives 8,—I write down 8; 6 the complement of 3 with respect to 9 added to 5 gives 11,— I write down 1 and carry 1; 3 the complement of 6 with respect to 9, plus 9, by reason of the 1 carried, gives 12,—I put down 2 and carry 1; lastly, 7 the complement of 2 with respect to 9 plus 8, on account of the 1 carried, gives 15,—I put down 5 and this time carry nothing, for the operation is completed, and the last 10 which was borrowed in the course of the operation must be rejected. In this manner we obtain the same remainder as above, 5218.

<small>Subtraction by complements.</small> The foregoing method is extremely convenient when the numbers are large; for in the common method of subtraction, where borrowing is necessary in subtracting single numbers from one another, mistakes are frequently made, whereas in the method with which we are here concerned we never borrow but simply carry, the subtraction being converted into addition. With regard to the complements they are discoverable at the merest glance, for every one knows that 3 is the complement of 7 with respect to 10, 4 the complement of 5 with respect to 9, etc. And as to the reason of the method, it too is quite palpable. The different complements taken together form the total complement of the number to be subtracted either with respect to 10 or 100 or 1000, etc., according as the number has 1, 2, 3 . . . figures; so that the operation performed is virtually equivalent to first adding 10, 100, 1000 . . . to the minuend and then taking the subtrahend from the minuend as so augmented. Whence it is likewise apparent why the 10 of the sum found by the last partial addition must be rejected.

As to multiplication, there are various abridged methods possible, based on the decimal system of numbers. In multiplying by 10, for example, we have, as we know, simply to add a cipher; in multiplying by 100 we add two ciphers; by 1000, three ciphers, etc. Consequently, to multiply by any aliquot part of 10, for example 5, we have simply to multiply by 10 and then divide by 2; to multiply by 25 we multiply by 100 and divide by 4, and so on for all the products of 5.

<small>Abridged multiplication.</small>

When decimal numbers are to be multiplied by decimal numbers, the general rule is to consider the two numbers as integers and when the operation is finished to mark off from the right to the left as many places in the product as there are decimal places in the multiplier and the multiplicand together. But in practice this rule is frequently attended with the inconvenience of unnecessarily lengthening the operation, for when we have numbers containing decimals these numbers are ordinarily exact only to a certain number of places, so that it is necessary to retain in the product only the decimal places of an equivalent order. For example, if the multiplicand and the multiplier each contain two places of decimals and are exact only to two decimal places, we should have in the product by the ordinary method four decimal places, the two last of which we should have to reject as useless and inexact. I shall give you now a method for obtaining in the product only just so many decimal places as you desire.

I observe first that in the ordinary method of multiplying we begin with the units of the multiplier which we multiply with the units of the multiplicand, and so

Inverted multiplication.

continue from the right to the left. But there is nothing compelling us to begin at the right of the multiplier. We may equally well begin at the left. And I cannot in truth understand why the latter method should not be preferred, since it possesses the advantage of giving at once the figures having the greatest value, and since, in the majority of cases where large numbers are multiplied together, it is just these last and highest places that concern us most; we frequently, in fact, perform multiplications only to find what these last figures are. And herein, be it parenthetically remarked, consists one of the great advantages in calculating by logarithms, which always give, be it in multiplication or division, in involution or evolution, the figures in the descending order of their value, beginning with the highest and proceeding from the left to the right.

By performing multiplication in this manner, no difference is caused in the total product. The sole distinction is, that by the new method the first line, the first partial product, is that which in the ordinary method is last, and the second partial product is that which in the ordinary method is next to the last, and so with the rest.

Where whole numbers are concerned and the exact product is required, it is indifferent which method we employ. But when decimal places are involved the prime essential is to have the figures of the whole numbers first in the product and to descend after-

ON THE OPERATIONS OF ARITHMETIC. 29

wards successively to the figures of the decimal parts, instead of, as in the ordinary method, beginning with the last decimal places and successively ascending to the figures forming the whole numbers.

In applying this method practically, we write the multiplier underneath the multiplicand so that the units' figure of the multiplier falls beneath the last figure of the multiplicand. We then begin with the last left-hand figure of the multiplier which we multiply as in the ordinary method by all the figures of the multiplicand, beginning with the last to the right and proceeding successively to the left; observing that the first figure of the product is to be placed underneath the figure with which we are multiplying, while the others follow in their successive order to the left. We proceed in the same manner with the second figure of the multiplier, likewise placing beneath this figure the first figure of the product, and so on with the rest. The place of the decimal point in these different products will be the same as in the multiplicand, that is to say, the units of the products will all fall in the same vertical line with those of the multiplicand and consequently those of the sum of all the products or of the total product will also fall in that line. In this manner it is an easy matter to calculate only as many decimal places as we wish. I give below an example of this method in which the multiplicand is 437.25 and the multiplier 27.34 :

Approximate multiplication.

The new method exemplified.

$$\begin{array}{r|l} & 437.25 \\ & 27.34 \\ \hline 8745 & 0 \\ 3060 & 75 \\ 131 & 17\ 5 \\ 17 & 49\ 00 \\ \hline 11954 & 41\ 50 \end{array}$$

I have written all the decimals in the product, but it is easy to see how we may omit calculating the decimals which we wish to neglect. The vertical line is used to mark more distinctly the place of the decimal point.

The preceding rule appears to me simpler and more natural than that which is attributed to Oughtred and which consists in writing the multiplier underneath the multiplicand in the reverse order.

There is one more point, finally, to be remarked in connexion with the multiplication of numbers containing decimals, and that is that we may alter the place of the decimal point of either number at will. For seeing that moving the decimal point from the right to the left in one of the numbers is equivalent to dividing the number by 10, by 100, or by 1000..., and that moving the decimal point back in the other number the same number of places from the left to the right is tantamount to multiplying that number by 10, 100, or 1000, ... , it follows that we may push the decimal point forward in one of the numbers as many places as we please provided we move it back in the other number the same number of places, without in any wise altering the product. In this way we can always so arrange it that one of the two numbers shall contain no decimals—which simplifies the question.

Division is susceptible of a like simplification, for since the quotient is not altered by multiplying or dividing the dividend and the divisor by the same number, it follows that in division we may move the decimal point of both numbers forwards or backwards as many places as we please, provided we move it the same distance in each case. Consequently, we can always reduce the divisor to a whole number—which facilitates infinitely the operation for the reason that when there are decimal places in the dividend only, we may proceed with the division by the common method and neglect all places giving decimals of a lower order than those we desire to take account of.

Division of decimals.

You know the remarkable property of the number 9, whereby if a number be divisible by 9 the sum of its digits is also divisible by 9. This property enables us to tell at once, not only whether a number is divisible by 9 but also what is its remainder from such division. For we have only to take the sum of its digits and to divide that sum by 9, when the remainder will be the same as that of the original number divided by 9.

The demonstration of the foregoing proposition is not difficult. It reposes upon the fact that the numbers 10 less 1, 100 less 1, 1000 less 1, . . . are all divisible by 9,—which seeing that the resulting numbers are 9, 99, 999, . . . is quite obvious.

If, now, you subtract from a given number the sum of all its digits, you will have as your remainder the tens' digit multiplied by 9, the hundreds' digit multiplied by 99, the thousands' digit multiplied by 999, and so on,—a remainder which is plainly divisible by 9. Consequently, if the sum of the digits is divisible by 9, the original number itself will be so divisible, and if it is not divisible by 9 the original number likewise will not be divisible thereby. But the remainder in the one case will be the same as in the other.

Property of the number 9.

In the case of the number 9, it is evident immediately that 10 less 1, 100 less 1, . . . are divisible by 9; but algebra demonstrates that the property in question holds good for every number a. For it can be shown that

$$a-1,\ a^2-1,\ a^3-1,\ a^4-1,\ \ldots$$

are all quantities divisible by $a-1$, actual division giving the quotients

$$1,\ a+1,\ a^2+a+1,\ a^3+a^2+a+1,\ \ldots.$$

The conclusion is therefore obvious that the aforesaid property of the number 9 holds good in our decimal system of arithmetic because 9 is 10 less 1, and that in any other system founded upon the progression $a,\ a^2,\ a^3,\ \ldots$ the number $a-1$ would enjoy the same property. Thus in the duodecimal system it would be the number 11; and in this system every number, the sum of whose digits was divisible by 11, would also itself be divisible by that number.

The foregoing property of the number 9, now, admits of generalisation, as the following consideration will show. Since every number in our system is represented by the sum of certain terms of the progression 1, 10, 100, 1000, ..., each multiplied by one of the nine digits 1, 2, 3, 4, ... 9, it is easy to see that the remainder resulting from the division of any number by a given divisor will be equal to the sum of the remainders resulting from the division of the terms 1, 10, 100, 1000, ... by that divisor, each multiplied by the digit showing how many times the corresponding term has been taken. Hence, generally, if the given divisor be called D, and if m, n, p, ... be the remainders of the division of the numbers 1, 10, 100, 1000 by D, the remainder from the division of any number whatever N, of which the characters proceeding from the right to the left are a, b, c, ..., by D will obviously be equal to

$$ma + nb + pc + \ldots$$

Property of the number 9 generalised.

Accordingly, if for a given divisor D we know the remainders m, n, p, ..., which depend solely upon that divisor and which are always the same for the same divisor, we have only to write the remainders underneath the original number, proceeding from the right to the left, and then to find the different products of

Theory of remainders

each digit of the number by the digit which is underneath it. The sum of all these products will be the total remainder resulting from the division of the proposed number by the same divisor D. And if the sum found is greater than D, we can proceed in the same manner to seek its remainder from division by D, and so on until we arrive finally at a remainder which is less than D, which will be the true remainder sought. It follows from this that the proposed number cannot be exactly divisible by the given divisor unless the last remainder found by this method is zero.

The remainders resulting from the division of the terms 1, 10, 100, ... 1000, by 9 are always unity. Hence, the sum of the digits of any number whatever is the remainder resulting from the division of that number by 9. The remainders resulting from the division of the same terms by 8 are 1, 2, 4, 0, 0, 0, ... We shall obtain, accordingly, the remainder resulting from dividing any number by 8, by taking the sum of the first digit to the right, the second digit next thereto to the left multiplied by 2, and the third digit multiplied by 4.

The remainders resulting from the divisions of the terms 1, 10, 100, 1000, . . . by 7 are 1, 3, 2, 6, 4, 5, 1, 3, . . . , where the same remainders continually recur in the same order. If I have, now, the number 13527541 to be divided by 7, I write it thus with the above remainders underneath it:

$$\begin{array}{r} 13527541 \\ 31546231 \\ \hline 1 \\ 12 \\ 10 \\ 42 \\ 8 \\ 25 \\ 3 \\ 3 \\ \hline 104 \\ 231 \\ \hline 4 \\ 0 \\ 2 \\ \hline 6 \end{array}$$

Test of divisibility by 7.

Taking the partial products and adding them, I obtain 104, which would be the remainder from the division of the given number by 7, were it not greater than the divisor. I accordingly repeat the operation with this remainder, and find for my second remainder 6, which is the real remainder in question.

I have still to remark with regard to the preceding remainders and the multiplications which result from them, that they may be simplified by introducing negative remainders in the place of remainders which are greater than half the divisor, and to accomplish this we have simply to subtract the divisor from each of such remainders. We obtain thus, instead of the remainders 6, 5, 4, the following:

$$-1, -2, -3.$$

The remainders for the divisor 7, accordingly, are

1, 3, 2, —1, —3, —2, 1, 3, . . .

and so on to infinity.

Negative remainders The preceding example, then, takes the following form :

$$\begin{array}{r} 13527541 \\ 31231231 \\ \hline 7\;1 \\ 6\;12 \\ \underline{10\;10} \\ 23\;\;3 \\ \underline{3} \\ 29 \\ \text{subtract } \underline{23} \\ 6 \end{array}$$

I have placed a bar beneath the digits which are to be taken negatively, and I have subtracted the sum of the products of these numbers by those above them from the sum of the other products.

The whole question, therefore, resolves itself into finding for every divisor the remainders resulting from dividing 1, 10, 100, 1000 by that divisor. This can be readily done by actual division; but it can be accomplished more simply by the following consideration. If r be the remainder from the division of 10 by a given divisor, r^2 will be the remainder from the division of 100, the square of 10, by that divisor; and consequently it will be necessary merely to subtract the given divisor from r^2 as many times as is requisite to obtain a positive or negative remainder less than

ON THE OPERATIONS OF ARITHMETIC. 37

half of that divisor. Let s be that remainder; we shall then only have to multiply s by r, the remainder from the division of 10, to obtain the remainder from the division of 1000 by the given divisor, because 1000 is 100×10, and so on.

For example, dividing 10 by 7 we have a remainder of 3; hence, the remainder from dividing 100 by 7 will be 9, or, subtracting from 9 the given divisor 7, 2. The remainder from dividing 1000 by 7, then, will be the product of 2 by 3 or 6, or, subtracting the divisor, 7, -1. Again, the remainder from dividing 10,000 by 7 will be the product of -1 and 3, or -3, and so on.

Let us now take the divisor 11. The remainder from dividing 1 by 11 is 1, from dividing 10 by 11 is 10, or, subtracting the divisor, -1. The remainder from dividing 100 by 11, then, will be the square of -1, or 1; from dividing 1000 by 11 it will be 1 multiplied by -1 or -1 again, and so on forever, the remainders forming the infinite series

$$1, -1, 1, -1, 1, -1, \ldots$$

Test of divisibility by 11.

Hence results the remarkable property of the number 11, that if the digits of any number be alternately added and subtracted, that is to say, if we take the sum of the first, the third, and the fifth, etc., and subtract from it the sum of the second, the fourth, the sixth, etc., we shall obtain the remainder which results from dividing that number by the number 11.

Theory of remainders

The preceding theory of remainders is fraught with remarkable consequences, and has given rise to many ingenious and difficult investigations. We can demonstrate, for example, that if the divisor is a prime number, the remainders of any progression 1, a, a^2, a^3, a^4, ... form periods which will recur continually to infinity, and all of which, like the first, begin with unity; in such wise that when unity reappears among the remainders we may continue them to infinity by simply repeating the remainders which precede. It has also been demonstrated that these periods can only contain a number of terms which is equal to the divisor less 1 or to an aliquot part of the divisor less 1. But we have not yet been able to determine *à priori* this number for any divisor whatever.

As to the utility of this method for finding the remainder resulting from dividing a given number by a given divisor, it is frequently very useful when one has several numbers to divide by the same number, and it is required to prepare a table of the remainders. While as to division by 9 and 11, since that is very simple, it can be employed as a check upon multiplication and division. Having found the remainders from dividing the multiplicand and the multiplier by either of these numbers it is simply necessary to take the product of the two remainders so resulting, from which, after subtracting the divisor as many times as is requisite, we shall obtain the remainder from dividing their product by the given divisor,—a remainder which should agree with the remainder obtained from treating the actual product in this manner. And since in division the dividend less the remainder should be equal to the product of the divisor and the quotient, the same check may also be applied here to advantage. *Checks on multiplication and division.*

The supposition which I have just made that the product of the remainders from dividing two numbers by the same divisor is equal to the remainder from dividing the product of these numbers by the same divisor is easily proved, and I here give a general demonstration of it.

Let M and N be two numbers, D the divisor, p and q the quotients, and r, s the two remainders. We shall plainly have

$$M = pD + r, \quad N = qD + s,$$

from which by multiplying we obtain

$$MN = pqD^2 + spD + rqD + rs;$$

where it will be seen that all the terms are divisible by D with the exception of the last, rs, whence it follows that rs will be the remainder from dividing MN by D. It is further evident that if any multiple whatever of D, as mD, be subtracted from rs, the result $rs - mD$ will also be the remainder from dividing MN by D. For, putting the value of MN in the following form:

$$pqD^2 + spD + rqD + mD + rs - mD,$$

it is obvious that the remaining terms are all divisible

40 ON THE OPERATIONS OF ARITHMETIC.

by D. And this remainder $rs-mD$ can always be made less than D, or, by employing negative remainders, less even than $\dfrac{D}{2}$.

Evolution.

This is all that I have to say upon multiplication and division. I shall not speak of the *extraction of roots*. The rule is quite simple for square roots; it leads directly to its goal; trials are unnecessary. As to cube and higher roots, the occasion rarely arises for extracting them, and when it does arise the extraction can be performed with great facility by means of logarithms, where the degree of exactitude can be carried to as many decimal places as the logarithms themselves have decimal places. Thus, with seven-place logarithms we can extract roots having seven figures, and with the large tables where the logarithms have been calculated to ten decimal places we can obtain even ten figures of the result.

One of the most important operations in arithmetic is the so-called *rule of three*, which consists in finding the fourth term of a proportion of which the first three terms are given.

In the ordinary text-books of arithmetic this rule has been unnecessarily complicated, having been divided into simple, direct, inverse, and compound rules of three. In general it is sufficient to comprehend the conditions of the problem thoroughly, for the common rule of three is always applicable where a quantity increases or diminishes in the same proportion as another. For example, the price of things augments in proportion to the quantity of the things, so that the quantity of the thing being doubled, the price also will be doubled, and so on. Similarly, the amount of work done increases proportionally to the number of persons employed. Again, things may increase simultaneously in two different proportions. For example, the quantity of work done increases with the number of the persons employed, and also with the time during which they are employed. Further, there are things that decrease as others increase.

<small>Rule of three.</small>

Now all this may be embraced in a single, simple proposition. If a quantity increases both in the ratio in which one or several other quantities increase and in that in which one or several other quantities decrease, it is the same thing as saying that the proposed quantity increases proportionally to the product of the quantities which increase with it, divided by the product of the quantities which simultaneously decrease. For example, since the quantity of work done increases proportionally with the number of laborers and with the time during which they work and since it diminishes in proportion as the work becomes more difficult, we may say that the result is proportional to the number of laborers multiplied by the number measuring the time during which they labor, divided by the number which measures or expresses the difficulty of the work.

The further fact should not be lost sight of that

the rule of three is properly applicable only to things which increase in a constant ratio. For example, it is assumed that if a man does a certain amount of work in one day, two men will do twice that amount in one day, three men three times that amount, four men four times that amount, etc. In reality this is not the case, but in the rule of proportion it is assumed to be such, since otherwise we should not be able to employ it.

<small>Applicability of the rule of three.</small>

When the law of augmentation or diminution varies, the rule of three is not applicable, and the ordinary methods of arithmetic are found wanting. We must then have recourse to algebra.

A cask of a certain capacity empties itself in a certain time. If we were to conclude from this that a cask of double that capacity would empty itself in double the time, we should be mistaken, for it will empty itself in a much shorter time. The law of efflux does not follow a constant ratio but a variable ratio which diminishes with the quantity of liquid remaining in the cask.

We know from mechanics that the spaces traversed by a body in uniform motion bear a constant ratio to the times elapsed. If we travel one mile in one hour, in two hours we shall travel two miles. But the spaces traversed by a falling stone are not in a fixed ratio to the time. If it falls sixteen feet in the first second, it will fall forty-eight feet in the second second.

The rule of three is applicable when the ratios are

constant only. And in the majority of affairs of ordinary life constant ratios are the rule. In general, the price is always proportional to the quantity, so that if a given thing has a certain value, two such things will have twice that value, three three times that value, four four times that value, etc. It is the same with the product of labor relatively to the number of laborers and to the duration of the labor. Nevertheless, cases occur in which we may be easily led into error. If two horses, for example, can pull a load of a certain weight, it is natural to suppose that four horses could pull a load of double that weight, six horses a load of three times that weight. Yet, strictly speaking, such is not the case. For the inference is based upon the assumption that the four horses pull alike in amount and direction, which in practice can scarcely ever be the case. It so happens that we are frequently led in our reckonings to results which diverge widely from reality. But the fault is not the fault of mathematics; for mathematics always gives back to us exactly what we have put into it. The ratio was constant according to the supposition. The result is founded upon that supposition. If the supposition is false the result is necessarily false. Whenever it has been attempted to charge mathematics with inexactitude, the accusers have simply attributed to mathematics the error of the calculator. False or inexact data having been employed by him, the result also has been necessarily false or inexact.

Theory and practice.

Alligation. Among the other rules of arithmetic there is one called *alligation* which deserves special consideration from the numerous applications which it has. Although alligation is mainly used with reference to the mingling of metals by fusion, it is yet applied generally to mixtures of any number of articles of different values which are to be compounded into a whole of a like number of parts having a mean value. The rule of alligation, or mixtures, accordingly, has two parts.

In one we seek the mean and common value of each part of the mixture, having given the number of the parts and the particular value of each. In the second, having given the total number of the parts and their mean value, we seek the composition of the mixture itself, or the proportional number of parts of each ingredient which must be mixed or alligated together.

Let us suppose, for example, that we have several bushels of grain of different prices, and that we are desirous of knowing the mean price. The mean price must be such that if each bushel were of that price the total price of all the bushels together would still be the same. Whence it is easy to see that to find the mean price in the present case we have first simply to find the total price and to divide it by the number of bushels.

In general if we multiply the number of things of each kind by the value of the unit of that kind and then divide the sum of all these products by the total number of things, we shall have the mean value, because that value multiplied by the number of the things will again give the total value of all the things taken together.

This mean or average value as it is called, is of great utility in almost all the affairs of life. Whenever we arrive at a number of different results, we always like to reduce them to a mean or average expression which will yield the same total result.

Mean values.

You will see when you come to the calculus of probabilities that this science is almost entirely based upon the principle we are discussing.

The registration of births and deaths has rendered possible the construction of so-called *tables of mortality* which show what proportion of a given number of children born at the same time or in the same year survive at the end of one year, two years, three years, etc. So that we may ask upon this basis what is the mean or average value of the life of a person at any given age. If we look up in the tables the number of people living at a certain age, and then add to this the number of persons living at all subsequent ages, it is clear that this sum will give the total number of years which all living persons of the age in question have still to live. Consequently, it is only necessary to divide this sum by the number of living persons of a certain age in order to obtain the average duration of life of such persons, or better, the number of years which each person must live that the total number of years lived by all shall be the same and that each person shall have lived an equal number. It has been found in this manner by taking the mean of the results of different tables of mortality, that for an infant one year old the average duration of life is about 40 years; for a child ten years old it is still 40 years; for 20 it is 34; for 30 it is 26; for 40 it is 23; for 50 it is 17; for 60 it is 12; for 70, 8; and for 80, 5.

<small>Probability of life.</small>

To take another example, a number of different experiments are made. Three experiments have given 4 as a result; two experiments have given 5; and one has given 6. To find the mean we multiply 4 by 3, 5 by 2, and 1 by 6, add the products which gives 28, and divide 28 by the number of experiments or 6, which gives $4\tfrac{2}{3}$ as the mean result of all the experiments.

But it will be apparent that this result can be regarded as exact only upon the condition of our having supposed that the experiments were all conducted with equal precision. But it is impossible that such could have been the case, and it is consequently imperative to take account of these inequalities, a requirement which would demand a far more complicated calculus than that which we have employed, and one which is now engaging the attention of mathematicians.

The foregoing is the substance of the first part of the rule of alligation; the second part is the opposite of the first. Given the mean value, to find how much must be taken of each ingredient to produce the required mean value.

The problems of the first class are always determinate, because, as we have just seen, the number of units of each ingredient has simply to be multiplied by the value of each ingredient and the sum of all these products divided by the number of the ingredients.

Alternate alligation.

The problems of the second class, on the other hand, are always indeterminate. But the condition that only positive whole numbers shall be admitted in the result serves to limit the number of the solutions.

Suppose that we have two kinds of things, that the value of the unit of one kind is a, and that of the unit of the second is b, and that it is required to find how many units of the first kind and how many units of the second must be taken to form a mixture or whole of which the mean value shall be m.

Call x the number of units of the first kind that must enter into the mixture, and y the number of units of the second kind. It is clear that ax will be the value of the x units of the first kind, and by the value of the y units of the second. Hence $ax + by$ will be the total value of the mixture. But the mean value of the mixture being by supposition m, the sum $x + y$ of the units of the mixture multiplied by m, the mean value of each unit, must give the same total value. We shall have, therefore, the equation

$$ax + by = mx + my.$$

Transposing to one side the terms multiplied by x and to the other the terms multiplied by y, we obtain:

Two ingredients.

$$(a-m)x = (m-b)y$$

and dividing by $a-m$ we get

$$x = \frac{(m-b)y}{a-m},$$

whence it appears that the number y may be taken at pleasure, for whatever be the value given to y, there will always be a corresponding value of x which will satisfy the problem.

Such is the general solution which algebra gives. But if the condition be added that the two numbers x and y shall be integers, then y may not be taken at pleasure. In order to see how we can satisfy this last condition in the simplest manner, let us divide the last equation by y, and we shall have

$$\frac{x}{y} = \frac{m-b}{a-m}.$$

For x and y both to be positive, it is necessary that the quantities

$$m-b \text{ and } a-m$$

should both have the same sign; that is to say, if a is greater or less than m, then conversely b must be less or greater than m; or again, m must lie between a and b, which is evident from the condition of the problem. Suppose a, then, to be the greater and b

the smaller of the two prices. It remains to find the value of the fraction

$$\frac{m-b}{a-m},$$

<small>Rule of mixtures.</small>

which if necessary is to be reduced to its lowest terms. Let $\frac{B}{A}$ be that fraction reduced to its lowest terms. It is clear that the simplest solution will be that in which

$$x = B \text{ and } y = A.$$

But since a fraction is not altered by multiplying its numerator and denominator by the same number, it is clear that we may also take $x = nB$ and $y = nA$, n being any number whatever, provided it is an integer, for by supposition x and y must be integers. And it is easy to prove that these expressions of x and y are the only ones which will resolve the proposed problem. According to the ordinary rule of mixtures, x, the quantity of the dearer ingredient, is made equal to $m-b$, the excess of the average price above the lower price, and y the quantity of the cheaper ingredient is made equal to $a-m$, the excess of the higher price above the average price,—a rule which is contained directly in the general solution above given.

Suppose, now, that instead of two kinds of things, we have three kinds, the values of which beginning with the highest are a, b, and c. Let x, y, z be the quantities which must be taken of each to form a mixture or compound having the mean value m. The sum of the values of the three quantities x, y, z will then be

$$ax + by + cz.$$

But this total value must be the same as that produced if all the individual values were m, in which case the total value is obviously

Three ingredients.

$$mx + my + mz.$$

The following equation, therefore, must be satisfied:
$$ax + by + cz = mx + my + mz,$$
or, more simply,
$$(a-m)x + (b-m)y + (c-m)z = 0.$$
Since there are three unknown quantities in this equation, two of them may be taken at pleasure. But if the condition is that they shall be expressed by positive integers, it is to be observed first that the numbers
$$a-m \text{ and } m-c$$
are necessarily positive; so that putting the equation in the form
$$(a-m)x - (m-c)z = (m-b)y,$$
the question resolves itself into finding two multiples of the given numbers
$$a-m \text{ and } m-c$$
whose difference shall be equal to $(m-b)y$.

This question is always resolvable in whole numbers whatever the given numbers be of which we seek the multiples, and whatever be the difference between these multiples. As it is sufficiently remarkable in itself and may be of utility in many emergencies, we shall give here a general solution of it, derived from the properties of continued fractions.

Let M and N be two whole numbers. Of these numbers two multiples xM, zN are sought whose difference is given and equal to D. The following equation will then have to be satisfied

General solution.

$$xM - zN = D,$$

where x and z by supposition are whole numbers. In the first place, it is plain that if M and N are not prime to each other, the number D is divisible by the greatest common divisor of M and N; and the division having been performed, we should have a similar equation in which the numbers M and N are prime to each other, so that we are at liberty always to suppose them reduced to that condition. I now observe that if we know the solution of the equation for the case in which the number D is equal to $+1$ or -1, we can deduce the solution of it for any value whatever of D. For example, suppose that we know two multiples of M and N, say pM and qN, the difference of which $pM - qN$ is equal to ± 1. Then obviously we shall merely have to multiply both these multiples by the number D to obtain a difference equal to $\pm D$. For, multiplying the preceding equation by D, we have

$$pDM - qDN = \pm D;$$

and subtracting the latter equation from the original equation

$$xM - zN = D,$$

or adding it, according as the term D has the sign $+$ or $-$ before it, we obtain

$$(x \mp pD)M - (z \mp qD)N = 0,$$

which gives at once, as we saw above in the rule for the mixture of two different ingredients,

Development.

$$x \mp pD = nN, \ z \mp qD = nM,$$

n being any number whatever. So that we have generally

$$x = nN \pm 'pD \text{ and } z = nM \pm qD$$

where n is any whole number, positive or negative. It remains merely to find two numbers p and q such that

$$pM - qN = \pm 1.$$

Now this question is easily resolvable by continued fractions. For we have seen in treating of these fractions that if the fraction $\frac{M}{N}$ be reduced to a continued fraction, and all the successive fractions approximating to its value be calculated, the last of these successive fractions being the fraction $\frac{M}{N}$ itself, then the series of fractions so reached is such that the difference between any two consecutive fractions is always equal to a fraction of which the numerator is unity and the denominator the product of the two denominators. For example, designating by $\frac{K}{L}$ the fraction which immediately precedes the last fraction $\frac{M}{N}$ we obtain necessarily

$$LM - KN = 1 \text{ or } -1,$$

according as $\frac{M}{N}$ is greater or less than $\frac{K}{L}$, in other words, according as the place occupied by the last fraction $\frac{M}{N}$ in the series of fractions successively approximating to its value is even or odd; for, the first fraction of the approximating series is always smaller, the second larger, the third smaller, etc., than the original fraction which is identical with the last fraction of the series. Making, therefore,

$$p = L \text{ and } q = K,$$

the problem of the two multiples will be resolved in all its generality.

Resolution by continued fractions.

It is now clear that in order to apply the foregoing solution to the initial question regarding alligation we have simply to put

$$M = a - m, \ N = m - c, \text{ and } D = (m - b)y;$$

so that the number y remains undetermined and may be taken at pleasure, as may also the number N which appears in the expressions for x and z.

LECTURE III.

ON ALGEBRA, PARTICULARLY THE RESOLUTION OF EQUATIONS OF THE THIRD AND FOURTH DEGREE.

Algebra among the ancients.

ALGEBRA is a science almost entirely due to the moderns. I say almost entirely, for we have one treatise from the Greeks, that of Diophantus, who flourished in the third* century of the Christian era. This work is the only one which we owe to the ancients in this branch of mathematics. When I speak of the ancients I speak of the Greeks only, for the Romans have left nothing in the sciences, and to all appearances did nothing.

Diophantus may be regarded as the inventor of algebra.† From a word in his preface, or rather in his letter of dedication, (for the ancient geometers were wont to address their productions to certain of their friends, a practice exemplified in the prefaces of Apollonius and Archimedes), from a word in his preface, I say, we learn that he was the first to occupy himself

---

*The period is uncertain. Some say in the fourth century. See Cantor, *Geschichte der Mathematik*, 2nd. ed., Vol. 1., p. 434.—*Trans.*

† On this point, see *Appendix*, p. 151.—*Trans.*

with that branch of arithmetic which has since been called algebra.

His work contains the first elements of this science. He employed to express the unknown quantity a Greek letter which corresponds to our st* and which has been replaced in the translations by N. To express the known quantities he employed numbers solely, for algebra was long destined to be restricted entirely to the solution of numerical problems. We find, however, that in setting up his equations consonantly with the conditions of the problem he uses the known and the unknown quantities alike. And herein consists virtually the essence of algebra, which is to employ unknown quantities, to calculate with them as we do with known quantities, and to form from them one or several equations from which the value of the unknown quantities can be determined. Although the work of Diophantus contains indeterminate problems almost exclusively, the solution of which he seeks in rational numbers,—problems which have been designated after him *Diophantine problems*,—we nevertheless find in his work the solution of a number of determinate problems of the first degree, and even of such as involve several unknown quantities. In the latter case, however, the author invariably has recourse to particular artifices for reducing the problem to a single unknown quantity,—which is not difficult. He gives,

<small>Diophantus</small>

---

*According to a recent conjecture, the character in question is an abbreviation of αρ the first letters of ἀριθμός, *number*, the appellation technically applied by Diophantus to the unknown quantity.—*Trans.*

also, the solution of *equations of the second degree*, but is careful so to arrange them that they never assume the affected form containing the square and the first power of the unknown quantity.

He proposed, for example, the following question which involves the general theory of equations of the second degree:

<small>Equations of the second degree.</small>

To find two numbers the sum and the product of which are given.

If we call the sum a and the product b we have at once, by the theory of equations, the equation

$$x^2 - ax + b = 0.$$

Diophantus resolves this problem in the following manner. The sum of the two numbers being given, he seeks their difference, and takes the latter as the unknown quantity. He then expresses the two numbers in terms of their sum and difference,—the one by half the sum plus half the difference, the other by half the sum less half the difference,—and he has then simply to satisfy the other condition by equating their product to the given number. Calling the given sum a, the unknown difference x, one of the numbers will be $\frac{a+x}{2}$ and the other will be $\frac{a-x}{2}$. Multiplying these together we have $\frac{a^2-x^2}{4}$. The term containing x is here eliminated, and equating the quantity last obtained to the given product, we have the simple equation

$$\frac{a^2-x^2}{4} = b,$$

from which we obtain
$$x^2 = a^2 - 4b,$$
and from the latter
$$x = \sqrt{a^2 - 4b}.$$

Diophantus resolves several other problems of this class. By appropriately treating the sum or difference as the unknown quantity he always arrives at an equation in which he has only to extract a square root to reach the solution of his problem. *Other problems solved by Diophantus.*

But in the books which have come down to us (for the entire work of Diophantus has not been preserved) this author does not proceed beyond equations of the second degree, and we do not know if he or any of his successors (for no other work on this subject has been handed down from antiquity) ever pushed their researches beyond this point.

I have still to remark in connexion with the work of Diophantus that he enunciated the principle that $+$ and $-$ give $-$ in multiplication, and $-$ and $-$, $+$, in the form of a definition. But I am of opinion that this is an error of the copyists, since he is more likely to have considered it as an axiom, as did Euclid some of the principles of geometry. However that may be, it will be seen that Diophantus regarded the rule of the signs as a self-evident principle not in need of demonstration.

The work of Diophantus is of incalculable value from its containing the first germs of a science which because of the enormous progress which it has since made constitutes one of the chiefest glories of the human intellect. Diophantus was not known in Europe until the end of the sixteenth century, the first translation having been a wretched one by Xylander made in 1575 and based upon a manuscript found about the middle of the sixteenth century in the Vatican library, where it had probably been carried from Greece when the Turks took possession of Constantinople.

Translations of Diophantus

Bachet de Méziriac, one of the earliest members of the French Academy, and a tolerably good mathematician for his time, subsequently published (1621) a new translation of the work of Diophantus accompanied by lengthy commentaries, now superfluous. Bachet's translation was afterwards reprinted with observations and notes by Fermat, one of the most celebrated mathematicians of France, who flourished about the middle of the seventeenth century, and of whom we shall have occasion to speak in the sequel for the important discoveries which he has made in analysis. Fermat's edition bears the date of 1670.*

It is much to be desired that good translations should be made, not only of the work of Diophantus, but also of the small number of other mathematical works which the Greeks have left us.†

---

*There have since been published a new critical edition of the text by M. Paul Tannery (Leipsic, 1893), and two German translations, one by O. Schulz (Berlin, 1822) and one by G. Wertheim (Leipsic, 1890). Fermat's notes on Diophantus have been republished in Vol. I. of the new edition of Fermat's works (Paris, Gauthier-Villars et Fils, 1891).—*Trans.*

† Since Lagrange's time this want has been partly supplied. Not to mention Euclid, we have, for example, of Archimedes the German translation of Nizze (Stralsund, 1824) and the French translation of Peyrard (Paris, 1807); of

Prior to the discovery and publication of Diophantus, however, algebra had already found its way into Europe. Towards the end of the fifteenth century there appeared in Venice a work by an Italian Franciscan monk named Lucas Paciolus on arithmetic and geometry in which the elementary rules of algebra were stated. This book was published (1494) in the early days of the invention of printing, and the fact that the name of *algebra* was given to the new science shows clearly that it came from the Arabs. It is true that the signification of this Arabic word is still disputed, but we shall not stop to discuss such matters, for they are foreign to our purpose. Let it suffice that the word has become the name for a science that is universally known, and that there is not the slightest ambiguity concerning its meaning, since up to the present time it has never been employed to designate anything else.

<small>Algebra among the Arabs.</small>

We do not know whether the Arabs invented algebra themselves or whether they took it from the Greeks.* There is reason to believe that they possessed the work of Diophantus, for when the ages of barbarism and ignorance which followed their first conquests had passed by, they began to devote themselves to the sciences and to translate into Arabic all the Greek works which treated of scientific subjects. It is reasonable to suppose, therefore, that they also

---

Apollonius, several translations; also modern translations of Hero, Ptolemy, Pappus, Theon, Proclus, and several others.

* See Appendix, p. 152.

translated the work of Diophantus and that the same work stimulated them to push their inquiries farther in this science.

<small>Algebra in Europe.</small> Be that as it may, the Europeans, having received algebra from the Arabs, were in possession of it one hundred years before the work of Diophantus was known to them. They made, however, no progress beyond equations of the first and second degree. In the work of Paciolus, which we mentioned above, the general resolution of equations of the second degree, such as we now have it, was not given. We find in this work simply rules, expressed in bad Latin verses, for resolving each particular case according to the different combinations of the signs of the terms of equation, and even these rules applied only to the case where the roots were real and positive. Negative roots were still regarded as meaningless and superfluous. It was geometry really that suggested to us the use of negative quantities, and herein consists one of the greatest advantages that have resulted from the application of algebra to geometry,—a step which we owe to Descartes.

In the subsequent period the resolution of *equations of the third degree* was investigated and the discovery for a particular case ultimately made by a mathematician of Bologna named Scipio Ferreus (1515).* Two other Italian mathematicians, Tartaglia and Cardan,

---

*The date is uncertain. Tartaglia gives 1506, Cardan 1515. Cantor prefers the latter.—*Trans.*

ON ALGEBRA.

subsequently perfected the solution of Ferreus and rendered it general for all equations of the third degree. At this period, Italy, which was the cradle of algebra in Europe, was still almost the sole cultivator of the science, and it was not until about the middle of the sixteenth century that treatises on algebra began to appear in France, Germany, and other countries. The works of Peletier and Buteo were the first which France produced in this science, the treatise of the former having been printed in 1554 and that of the latter in 1559.

Tartaglia (1500–1559).
Cardan (1501–1576).

Tartaglia expounded his solution in bad Italian verses in a work treating of divers questions and inventions printed in 1546, a work which enjoys the distinction of being one of the first to treat of modern fortifications by bastions.

About the same time (1545) Cardan published his treatise *Ars Magna*, or *Algebra*, in which he left scarcely anything to be desired in the resolution of equations of the third degree. Cardan was the first to perceive that equations had several roots and to distinguish them into positive and negative. But he is particularly known for having first remarked the so-called *irreducible case* in which the expression of the real roots appears in an imaginary form. Cardan convinced himself from several special cases in which the equation had rational divisors that the imaginary form did not prevent the roots from having a real value. But it remained to be proved that not only were the roots real in the irreducible case, but that it was impossible for all three together to be real except in that case. This proof was afterwards supplied by Vieta, and particularly by Albert Girard, from considerations touching the trisection of an angle.

<small>The irreducible case.</small> We shall revert later on to the *irreducible case of equations of the third degree*, not solely because it presents a new form of algebraical expressions which have found extensive application in analysis, but because it is constantly giving rise to unprofitable inquiries with a view to reducing the imaginary form to a real form and because it thus presents in algebra a problem which may be placed upon the same footing with the famous problems of the duplication of the cube and the squaring of the circle in geometry.

The mathematicians of the period under discussion were wont to propound to one another problems for solution. These problems were in the nature of public challenges and served to excite and to maintain in the minds of thinkers that fermentation which is necessary for the pursuit of science. The challenges in question were continued down to the beginning of the eighteenth century by the foremost mathematicians of Europe, and really did not cease until the rise of the Academies which fulfilled the same end in a manner even more conducive to the progress of science, partly by the union of the knowledge of their various members, partly by the intercourse which they maintained between them, and not least by the publication of their memoirs, which served to disseminate the new discoveries and observations among all persons interested in science.

The challenges of which we speak supplied in a measure the lack of Academies, which were not yet in existence, and we owe to these passages at arms many important discoveries in analysis. Such was the resolution of *equations of the fourth degree*, which was propounded in the following problem.

Biquadratic equations.

To find three numbers in continued proportion of which the sum is 10, and the product of the first two 6.

Generalising and calling the sum of the three numbers a, the product of the first two b, and the first two numbers themselves x, y, we shall have, first, $xy = b$. Owing to the continued proportion, the third number will then be expressed by $\frac{y^2}{x}$, so that the remaining condition will give

$$x + y + \frac{y^2}{x} = a.$$

From the first equation we obtain $x = \frac{b}{y}$, which substituted in the second gives

$$\frac{b}{y} + y + \frac{y^3}{b} = a,$$

Removing the fractions and arranging the terms, we get finally

$$y^4 + by^2 - aby + b^2 = 0,$$

an equation of the fourth degree with the second term missing.

According to Bombelli, of whom we shall speak

again, Louis Ferrari of Bologna resolved the problem by a highly ingenious method, which consists in dividing the equation into two parts both of which permit of the extraction of the square root. To do this it is necessary to add to the two numbers quantities whose determination depends on an equation of the third degree, so that the resolution of equations of the fourth degree depends upon the resolution of equations of the third and is therefore subject to the same drawbacks of the irreducible case.

Ferrari (1522-1565). Bombelli.

The *Algebra* of Bombelli was printed in Bologna in 1579* in the Italian language. It contains not only the discovery of Ferrari but also divers other important remarks on equations of the second and third degree and particularly on the theory of radicals by means of which the author succeeded in several cases in extracting the imaginary cube roots of the two binomials of the formula of the third degree in the irreducible case, so finding a perfectly real result and furnishing thus the most direct proof possible of the reality of this species of expressions.

Such is a succinct history of the first progress of algebra in Italy. The solution of equations of the third and fourth degree was quickly accomplished. But the successive efforts of mathematicians for over two centuries have not succeeded in surmounting the difficulties of the equation of the fifth degree.

*This was the second edition. The first edition appeared in Venice in 1572.—*Trans.*

ON ALGEBRA.

Yet these efforts are far from having been in vain. They have given rise to the many beautiful theorems which we possess on the formation of equations, on the character and signs of the roots, on the transformation of a given equation into others of which the roots may be formed at pleasure from the roots of the given equation, and finally, to the beautiful considerations concerning the metaphysics of the resolution of equations from which the most direct method of arriving at their solution, when possible, has resulted. All this has been presented to you in previous lectures and would leave nothing to be desired if it were but applicable to the resolution of equations of higher degree.

Theory of equations.

Vieta and Descartes in France, Harriot in England, and Hudde in Holland, were the first after the Italians whom we have just mentioned to perfect the theory of equations, and since their time there is scarcely a mathematician of note that has not applied himself to its investigation, so that in its present state this theory is the result of so many different inquiries that it is difficult in the extreme to assign the author of each of the numerous discoveries which constitute it.

I promised to revert to the irreducible case. To this end it will be necessary to recall the method which seems to have led to the original resolution of equations of the third degree and which is still employed in the majority of the treatises on algebra.

Let us consider the general equation of the third degree deprived of its second term, which can always be removed; in a word, let us consider the equation

Equations of the third degree.
$$x^3 + px + q = 0.$$

Suppose

$$x = y + z,$$

where y and z are two new unknown quantities, of which one consequently may be taken at pleasure and determined as we think most convenient. Substituting this value for x, we obtain *the transformed equation*

$$y^3 + 3y^2z + 3yz^2 + z^3 + p(y+z) + q = 0.$$

Factoring the two terms $3y^2z + 3yz^2$ we get

$$3yz(y+z),$$

and the transformed equation may be written as follows:

$$y^3 + z^3 + (3yz + p)(y+z) + q = 0.$$

Putting the factor multiplying $y + z$ equal to zero,— which is permissible owing to the two undetermined quantities involved,—we shall have the two equations

$$3yz + p = 0.$$

and

$$y^3 + z^3 + q = 0.$$

from which y and z can be determined. The means which most naturally suggests itself to this end is to take from the first equation the value of z,

$$z = -\frac{p}{3y},$$

and to substitute it in the second equation, removing the fractions by multiplication. So proceeding, we obtain the following equation of the sixth degree in y, called *the reduced equation*,

$$y^6 + qy^3 - \frac{p^3}{27} = 0,$$

The reduced equation.

which, since it contains two powers only of the unknown quantity, of which one is the square of the other, is resolvable after the manner of equations of the second degree and gives immediately

$$y^3 = -\frac{q}{2} + \sqrt{\frac{q^2}{4} + \frac{p^3}{27}},$$

from which, by extracting the cube root, we get

$$y = \sqrt[3]{-\frac{q}{2} + \sqrt{\frac{q^2}{4} + \frac{p^3}{27}}},$$

and finally,

$$x = y + z = y - \frac{p}{3y}$$

This expression for x may be simplified by remarking that the product of y by the radical

$$\sqrt[3]{-\frac{q}{2} - \sqrt{\frac{q^2}{4} + \frac{p^3}{27}}}$$

supposing all the quantities under the sign to be multiplied together, is

$$\sqrt[3]{-\frac{p^3}{27}} = -\frac{p}{3}.$$

The term $\frac{p}{3y}$, accordingly, takes the form

$$-\sqrt[3]{-\frac{q}{2} - \sqrt{\frac{q^2}{4} + \frac{p^3}{27}}},$$

and we have

$$x = \sqrt[3]{-\frac{q}{2} + \sqrt{\frac{q^2}{4} + \frac{p^3}{27}}} + \sqrt[3]{-\frac{q}{2} - \sqrt{\frac{q^2}{4} + \frac{p^3}{27}}},$$

an expression in which the square root underneath the cubic radical occurs in both its plus and minus forms and where consequently there can, on this score, be no occasion for ambiguity.

This last expression is known as the *Rule of Cardan*, and there has hitherto been no method devised for the resolution of equations of the third degree which does not lead to it. Since cubic radicals naturally present but a single value, it was long thought that Cardan's rule could give but one of the roots of the equation, and that in order to find the two others we must have recourse to the original equation and divide it by $x-a$, a being the first root found. The resulting quotient being an equation of the second degree may be resolved in the usual manner. The division in question is not only always possible, but it is also very easy to perform. For in the case we are considering the equation being

$$x^3 + px + q = 0,$$

if a is one of the roots we shall have

$$a^3 + pa + q = 0,$$

which subtracted from the preceding will give

$$x^3 - a^3 + p(x-a) = 0,$$

a quantity divisible by $x-a$ and having as its resulting quotient

$$x^2 + ax + a^2 + p = 0;$$

so that the new equation which is to be resolved for finding the two other roots will be

Marginal note: Cardan's rule.

$$x^2 + ax + a^2 + p = 0,$$

from which we have at once

$$x = -\frac{a}{2} \pm \sqrt{-p - \frac{3a^2}{4}}.$$

I see by the *Algebra* of Clairaut, printed in 1746, and by D'Alembert's article on the *Irreducible Case* in the first *Encyclopædia* that the idea referred to prevailed even in that period. But it would be the height of injustice to algebra to accuse it of not yielding results which were possessed of all the generality of which the question was susceptible. The sole requisite is to be able to read the peculiar hand-writing of algebra, and we shall then be able to see in it everything which by its nature it can be made to contain. In the case which we are considering it was forgotten that every cube root may have three values, as every square root has two. For the extraction of the cube root of a for example is merely equivalent to the resolution of the equation of the third degree $x^3 - a = 0$. Making $x = y \sqrt[3]{a}$, this last equation passes into the simpler form $y^3 - 1 = 0$, which has the root $y = 1$. Then dividing by $y - 1$ we have

$$y^2 + y + 1 = 0,$$

from which we deduce directly the two other roots

$$y = \frac{-1 \pm \sqrt{-3}}{2}.$$

These three roots, accordingly, are the three cube roots of unity, and they may be made to give the three cube roots of any other quantity a by multiplying them by the ordinary cube root of that quantity. It is the same with roots of the fourth, the fifth, and all the following degrees. For brevity, let us designate the two roots

The three cube roots of a quantity.

$$\frac{-1+\sqrt{-3}}{2} \quad \text{and} \quad \frac{-1-\sqrt{-3}}{2},$$

by m and n. It will be seen that they are imaginary, although their cube is real and equal to 1, as we may readily convince ourselves by raising them to the third power. We have, therefore, for the three cube roots of a,

$$\sqrt[3]{a}, \quad m\sqrt[3]{a}, \quad n\sqrt[3]{a}.$$

Now, in the resolution of the equation of the third degree above considered, on coming to the reduced expression $y^3 = A$, where for brevity we suppose

$$A = -\frac{q}{2} + \sqrt{\frac{q^2}{4} + \frac{p^3}{27}},$$

we deduced the following result only:

$$y = \sqrt[3]{A}.$$

But from what we have just seen, it is clear that we shall have not only

$$y = \sqrt[3]{A},$$

but also

$$y = m\sqrt[3]{A} \quad \text{and} \quad y = n\sqrt[3]{A}.$$

The root x of the equation of the third degree which we found equal to

$$y - \frac{p}{3y},$$

will therefore have the three following values

$\sqrt[3]{A} - \dfrac{p}{3\sqrt[3]{A}},\ m\sqrt[3]{A} - \dfrac{p}{3m\sqrt[3]{A}},\ n\sqrt[3]{A} - \dfrac{p}{3n\sqrt[3]{A}},$

which will be the three roots of the equation proposed. But making *The roots of equations of the third degree.*

$$B = -\dfrac{q}{2} - \sqrt{\dfrac{q^2}{4} + \dfrac{p^3}{27}},$$

it is clear that

$$AB = -\dfrac{p^3}{27},$$

whence

$$\sqrt[3]{A} \times \sqrt[3]{B} = -\dfrac{p}{3}.$$

Substituting $\sqrt[3]{B}$ for $-\dfrac{p}{3\sqrt[3]{A}}$, and remarking that $mn = 1$, and that consequently

$$\dfrac{1}{m} = n,\quad \dfrac{1}{n} = m,$$

the three roots which we are considering will be expressed as follows:

$$x = \sqrt[3]{A} + \sqrt[3]{B},\quad x = m\sqrt[3]{A} + n\sqrt[3]{B},$$
$$x = n\sqrt[3]{A} + m\sqrt[3]{B}.$$

We see, accordingly, that when properly understood the ordinary method gives the three roots directly, and gives three only. I have deemed it necessary to enter upon these slight details for the reason that if on the one hand the method was long taxed with being able to give but one root, on the other hand when it was seen that it really gave three it was thought that it should have given six, owing to the false employment of all the possible combinations of the three cubic roots of unity, viz., 1, m, n, with the two cubic radicals $\sqrt[3]{A}$ and $\sqrt[3]{B}$.

<small>A direct method of reaching the roots.</small>

We could have arrived directly at the results which we have just found by remarking that the two equations

$$y^3 + z^3 + q = 0 \text{ and } 3yz + p = 0$$

give

$$y^3 + z^3 = -q \text{ and } y^3 z^3 = -\frac{p^3}{27};$$

where it will be seen at once that y^3 and z^3 are the roots of an equation of the second degree of which the second term is q and the third $-\frac{p^3}{27}$. This equation, which is called *the reduced equation*, will accordingly have the form

$$u^2 + qu - \frac{p^3}{27} = 0;$$

and calling A and B its two roots we shall have immediately

$$y = \sqrt[3]{A}, \quad z = \sqrt[3]{B},$$

where it will be observed that A and B have the same values that they had in the previous discussion. Now, from what has gone before, we shall likewise have

$$y = m\sqrt[3]{A} \text{ or } y = n\sqrt[3]{A},$$

and the same will also hold good for z. But the equation

$$zy = -\frac{p}{3},$$

of which we have employed the cube only, limits these

values and it is easy to see that the restriction requires the three corresponding values of z to be

$$\sqrt[3]{B}, \; n\sqrt[3]{B}, \; m\sqrt[3]{B};$$

whence follow for the value of x, which is equal to $y + z$, the same three values which we found above.

As to the form of these values it is apparent, first, that so long as A and B are real quantities, one only of them can be real, for m and n are imaginary. They can consequently all three be real only in the case where the roots A and B of the reduced equation are imaginary, that is, when the quantity

The form of the roots

$$\frac{q^2}{4} + \frac{p^3}{27}$$

beneath the radical sign is negative, which happens only when p is negative and greater than

$$3\sqrt[3]{\frac{q^2}{4}}.$$

And this is the so-called *irreducible case*.

Since in this event

$$\frac{q^2}{4} + \frac{p^3}{27}$$

is a negative quantity, let us suppose it equal to $-g^2$, g being any real quantity whatever. Then making, for the sake of simplicity,

$$-\frac{q}{2} = f,$$

the two roots A and B of the reduced equation assume the form

$$A = f + g\sqrt{-1}, \; B = f - g\sqrt{-1}.$$

Now I say that if $\sqrt[3]{A} + \sqrt[3]{B}$, which is one of the roots of the equation of the third degree, is real, then the two other roots, expressed by

The reality of the roots

$$m\sqrt[3]{A} + n\sqrt[3]{B} \quad \text{and} \quad n\sqrt[3]{A} + m\sqrt[3]{B},$$

will also be real. Put

$$\sqrt[3]{A} = t, \quad \sqrt[3]{B} = u;$$

we shall have

$$t + u = h,$$

where h by hypothesis is a real quantity. Now,

$$tu = \sqrt[3]{AB} \quad \text{and} \quad AB = f^2 + g^2,$$

therefore

$$tu = \sqrt[3]{f^2 + g^2};$$

squaring the equation $t + u = h$ we have

$$t^2 + 2tu + u^2 = h^2;$$

from which subtracting $4tu$ we obtain

$$(t-u)^2 = h^2 - 4\sqrt[3]{f^2 + g^2}.$$

I observe that this quantity must necessarily be negative, for if it were positive and equal to k^2 we should have

$$(t-u)^2 = k^2,$$

whence

$$t - u = k.$$

Then since

$$t + u = h,$$

it would follow that

$$t = \frac{h+k}{2} \quad \text{and} \quad u = \frac{h-k}{2},$$

both of which are real quantities. But then t^3 and u^3 would also be real quantities, which is contrary to our hypothesis, since these quantities are equal to A and B, both of which are imaginary.

The quantity
$$h^2 - 4\sqrt[3]{f^2 + g^2}$$
therefore, is necessarily negative. Let us suppose it equal to $-k^2$; we shall have then
$$(t-u)^2 = -k^2,$$
and extracting the square root
$$t - u = k\sqrt{-1};$$
whence
$$t = \frac{h + k\sqrt{-1}}{2} = \sqrt[3]{A}, \quad u = \frac{h - k\sqrt{-1}}{2} = \sqrt[3]{B}.$$

The form of the two cubic radicals.

Such necessarily will be the form of the two cubic radicals
$$\sqrt[3]{f + g\sqrt{-1}} \text{ and } \sqrt[3]{f - g\sqrt{-1}},$$
a form at which we can arrive directly by expanding these roots according to the Newtonian theorem into series. But since proofs by series are apt to leave some doubt in the mind, I have sought to render the preceding discussion entirely independent of them.

If, therefore,
$$\sqrt[3]{A} + \sqrt[3]{B} = h,$$
we shall have
$$\sqrt[3]{A} = \frac{h + k\sqrt{-1}}{2} \text{ and } \sqrt[3]{B} = \frac{h - k\sqrt{-1}}{2}.$$

Now we have found above that
$$m = \frac{-1 + \sqrt{-3}}{2}, \quad n = \frac{-1 - \sqrt{-3}}{2};$$

wherefore, multiplying these quantities together, we have

$$m \sqrt[3]{A} + n \sqrt[3]{B} = \frac{-h + k\sqrt{3}}{2}$$

and

$$n \sqrt[3]{A} + m \sqrt[3]{B} = \frac{-h - k\sqrt{3}}{2},$$

<small>Condition of the reality of the roots.</small> which are real quantities. Consequently, if the root h is real, the two other roots also will be real in the irreducible case and they will be real in that case only.

But the invariable difficulty is, to demonstrate directly that

$$\sqrt[3]{f + g\sqrt{-1}} + \sqrt[3]{f - g\sqrt{-1}},$$

which we have supposed equal to h, is always a real quantity whatever be the values of f and g. In particular cases the demonstration can be effected by the extraction of the cube root, when that is possible. For example, if $f = 2$, $g = 11$, we shall find that the cube root of $2 + 11\sqrt{-1}$ will be $2 + \sqrt{-1}$, and similarly that the cube root of $2 - 11\sqrt{-1}$ will be $2 - \sqrt{-1}$, and the sum of the radicals will be 4. An infinite number of examples of this class may be constructed and it was through the consideration of such instances that Bombelli became convinced of the reality of the imaginary expression in the formula for the irreducible case. But forasmuch as the extraction of cube roots is in general possible only by means of series, we cannot arrive in this way at a general and direct demonstration of the proposition under consideration.

It is otherwise with square roots and with all roots of which the exponents are powers of 2. For example, if we have the expression

Extraction of the square roots of two imaginary binomials.

$$\sqrt{f+g\sqrt{-1}} + \sqrt{f-g\sqrt{-1}},$$

composed of two imaginary radicals, its square will be

$$2f + 2\sqrt{f^2 + g^2},$$

a quantity which is necessarily positive. Extracting the square root, so as to obtain the equivalent expression, we have

$$\sqrt{2f + 2\sqrt{f^2 + g^2}},$$

for the real value of the imaginary quantity we started with. But if instead of the sum we had had the difference between the two proposed imaginary radicals we should then have obtained for its square the following expression

$$2f - 2\sqrt{f^2 + g^2},$$

a quantity which is necessarily negative; and, taking the square root of the latter, we should have obtained the simple imaginary expression

$$\sqrt{2f - 2\sqrt{f^2 + g^2}}.$$

Further, if the quantity

$$\sqrt[4]{f+g\sqrt{-1}} + \sqrt[4]{f-g\sqrt{-1}}$$

were given, we should have, by squaring, the form

$$\sqrt{f+g\sqrt{-1}} + \sqrt{f-g\sqrt{-1}} + 2\sqrt[4]{f^2+g^2} =$$
$$\sqrt{2f + 2\sqrt{f^2+g^2}} + 2\sqrt[4]{f^2+g^2},$$

a real and positive quantity. Extracting the square

root of this expression we should obtain a real value for the original quantity; and so on for all the other remaining even roots. But if we should attempt to apply the preceding method to cubic radicals we should be led again to equations of the third degree in the irreducible case.

For example, let

<small>Extraction of the cube roots of two imaginary binomials.</small>
$$\sqrt[3]{f+g\sqrt{-1}} + \sqrt[3]{f-g\sqrt{-1}} = x.$$

Cubing, we get

$$2f + 3\sqrt[3]{f^2+g^2}\left(\sqrt[3]{f+g\sqrt{-1}} + \sqrt[3]{f-g\sqrt{-1}}\right) = x^3;$$

that is

$$2f + 3x\sqrt[3]{f^2+g^2} = x^3,$$

or, with the terms properly arranged,

$$x^3 - 3x\sqrt[3]{f^2+g^2} - 2f = 0,$$

the general formula of the irreducible case, for

$$\frac{1}{4}(2f)^2 + \frac{1}{27}\left(-3\sqrt[3]{f^2+g^2}\right)^3 = -g^2.$$

If $g = 0$ we shall have $x = 2\sqrt[3]{f}$. The sole *desideratum*, therefore, is to demonstrate that if g have any value whatever, x has a corresponding real value. Now the second last equation gives

$$\sqrt[3]{f^2+g^2} = \frac{x^3-2f}{3x}$$

and cubing we get

$$f^2 + g^2 = \frac{x^9 - 6x^6 f + 12 x^3 f^2 - 8f^3}{27 x^3},$$

whence

$$g^2 = \frac{x^9 - 6x^6 f - 15 x^3 f^2 - 8f^3}{27 x^3},$$

an equation which may be written as follows

$$g^2 = \frac{(x^3 - 8f)(x^3 + f)^2}{27\,x^3},$$

or, better, thus:

$$g^2 = \frac{1}{27}\left(1 - \frac{8f}{x^3}\right)(x^3 + f)^2.$$

It is plain from the last expression that g is zero when $x^3 = 8f$; further, that g constantly and uninterruptedly increases as x increases; for the factor $(x^3 + f)^2$ augments constantly, and the other factor $1 - \frac{8f}{x^3}$ also keeps increasing, seeing that as the denominator x^3 increases the negative part $\frac{8f}{x^3}$, which is originally equal to 1, keeps constantly growing less than 1. Therefore, if the value of x^3 be increased by insensible degrees from $8f$ to infinity, the value of g^2 will also augment by insensible and corresponding degrees from zero to infinity. And therefore, reciprocally, to every value of g^2 from zero to infinity there must correspond some value of x^3 lying between the limits of $8f$ and infinity, and since this is so whatever be the value of f we may legitimately conclude that, be the values of f and g what they may, the corresponding value of x^3 and consequently also of x is always real.

General theory of the reality of the roots

But how is this value of x to be assigned? It would seem that it can be represented only by an imaginary expression or by a series which is the development of an imaginary expression. Are we to regard this class of imaginary expressions, which correspond to real values, as constituting a new species of algebraical expressions which although they are not, like other expressions, susceptible of being numerically evaluated in the form in which they exist, yet possess the indisputable advantage—and this is the chief requisite—that they can be employed in the operations of algebra exactly as if they did not contain imaginary expressions. They further enjoy the advantage of having a wide range of usefulness in geometrical constructions, as we shall see in the theory of angular sections, so that they can always be exactly represented by lines; while as to their numerical value, we can always find it approximately and to any degree of exactness that we desire, by the approximate resolution of the equation on which they depend, or by the use of the common trigonometrical tables.

Imaginary expressions

It is demonstrated in geometry that if in a circle having the radius r an arc be taken of which the chord is c, and that if the chord of the third part of that arc be called x, we shall have for the determination of x the following equation of the third degree

$$x^3 - 3r^2 x + r^2 c = 0,$$

an equation which leads to the irreducible case since c is always necessarily less than $2r$, and which, owing to the two undetermined quantities r and c, may be taken as the type of all equations of this class. For, if we compare it with the general equation

$$x^3 + px + q = 0,$$

we shall have

$$r = \sqrt{-\frac{p}{3}} \text{ and } c = -\frac{3q}{p}$$

so that by trisecting the arc corresponding to the chord c in a circle of the radius r we shall obtain at once the value of a root x, which will be the chord of the third part of that arc. Now, from the nature of a circle the same chord c corresponds not only to the arc s but (calling the entire circumference u) also to the arcs

$$u-s,\ 2u+s,\ 3u-s,\ \ldots$$

Also the arcs

$$u+s,\ 2u-s,\ 3u+s,\ \ldots$$

have the same chord, but taken negatively, for on completing a full circumference the chords become zero and then negative, and they do not become positive again until the completion of the second circumference, as you may readily see. Therefore, the values of x are not only the chord of the arc $\frac{s}{3}$ but also the chords of the arcs

$$\frac{u-s}{3},\ \frac{2u+s}{3},$$

and these chords will be the three roots of the equation proposed. If we were to take the succeeding arcs which have the same chord c we should be led simply to the same roots, for the arc $3u-s$ would give the chord of $\frac{3u-s}{3}$, that is, of $u-\frac{s}{3}$, which we have already seen is the same as that of $\frac{s}{3}$, and so with the rest.

Trisection of an angle.

Since in the irreducible case the coefficient p is necessarily negative, the value of the given chord c will be positive or negative according as q is positive or negative. In the first case, we take for s the arc subtended by the positive chord $c = -\dfrac{3q}{p}$. The second case is reducible to the first by making x negative, whereby the sign of the last term is changed; so that if again we take for s an arc subtended by the positive chord $\dfrac{3q}{p}$, we shall have simply to change the sign of the three roots.

<small>Trigonometrical solution.</small>

Although the preceding discussion may be deemed sufficient to dispel all doubts concerning the nature of the roots of equations of the third degree, we propose adding to it a few reflexions concerning the method by which the roots are found. The method which we have propounded in the foregoing and which is commonly called *Cardan's method*, although it seems to me that we owe it to Hudde, has been frequently criticised, and will doubtless always be criticised, for giving the roots in the irreducible case in an imaginary form, solely because a supposition is here made which is contradictory to the nature of the equation. For the very gist of the method consists in its supposing the unknown quantity equal to two undetermined quantities $y+z$, in order to enable us afterwards to separate the resulting equation

$$y^3 + z^3 + (3yz + p)(y+z) + q = 0$$

into the two following:

$3yz + p = 0$ and $y^3 + z^3 + q = 0$.

Now, throwing the first of these into the form

$$y^3 z^3 = -\frac{p^3}{27}$$

The method of indeterminates.

it is plain that the question reduces itself to finding two numbers y^3 and z^3 of which the sum is $-q$ and the product $-\frac{p^3}{27}$, which is impossible unless the square of half the sum exceed the product, for the difference between these two quantities is equal to the square of half the difference of the numbers sought.

The natural conclusion was that it was not at all astonishing that we should reach imaginary expressions when proceeding from a supposition which it was impossible to express in numbers, and so some writers have been induced to believe that by adopting a different course the expression in question could be avoided and the roots all obtained in their real form.

Since pretty much the same objection can be advanced against the other methods which have since been found and which are all more or less based upon the method of indeterminates, that is, the introduction of certain arbitrary quantities to be determined so as to satisfy the conditions of the problem,—we propose to consider the question of the reality of the roots by itself and independently of any supposition whatever. Let us take again the equation

$$x^3 + px + q = 0;$$

and let us suppose that its three roots are *a, b, c*.

84 ON ALGEBRA.

By the theory of equations the left-hand side of the preceding expression is the product of three quantities

An independent consideration.

$$x-a, \quad x-b, \quad x-c,$$

which, multiplied together, give

$$x^3-(a+b+c)x^2+(ab+ac+bc)x-abc;$$

and comparing the corresponding terms, we have

$$a+b+c=0, \quad ab+ac+bc=p, \quad abc=-q.$$

As the degree of the equation is odd we may be certain, as you doubtless already know and in any event will clearly see from the lecture which is to follow, that it has necessarily one real root. Let that root be c. The first of the three equations which we have just found will then give

$$c=-a-b,$$

whence it is plain that $a+b$ is also necessarily a real quantity. Substituting the last value of c in the second and third equations, we have

$$ab-a^2-ab-ab-b^2=p, \quad -ab(a+b)=-q,$$

or

$$a^2+ab+b^2=-p, \quad ab(a+b)=q,$$

from which are to be found a and b. The last equation gives $ab=\dfrac{q}{a+b}$ from which I conclude that ab also is necessarily a real quantity. Let us consider now the quantity $\dfrac{q^2}{4}+\dfrac{p^3}{27}$ or, clearing of fractions, the quantity $27q^2+4p^3$, upon the sign of which the irreducible case depends. Substituting in this for p and q their value as given above in terms of a and b,

we shall find that when the necessary reductions are made the quantity in question is equal to the square of
$$2a^3 - 2b^3 + 3a^2b - 3ab^2$$

New view of the reality of the roots.

taken negatively; so that by changing the signs and extracting the square root we shall have
$$2a^3 - 2b^3 + 3a^2b - 3ab^2 = \sqrt{-27q^2 - 4p^3},$$

whence it is easy to infer that the two roots a and b cannot be real unless the quantity $27q^2 + 4p^3$ be negative. But I shall show that in that case, which is as we know the irreducible case, the two roots a and b are necessarily real. The quantity
$$2a^3 - 2b^3 + 3a^2b - 3ab^2$$
may be reduced to the form
$$(a-b)(2a^2 + 2b^2 + 5ab),$$
as multiplication will show. Now, we have already seen that the two quantities $a+b$ and ab are necessarily real, whence it follows that
$$2a^2 + 2b^2 + 5ab = 2(a+b)^2 + ab$$
is also necessarily real. Hence the other factor $a-b$ is also real when the radical $\sqrt{-27q^2 - 4p^3}$ is real. Therefore $a+b$ and $a-b$ being real quantities, it follows that a and b are real.

We have already derived the preceding theorems from the form of the roots themselves. But the present demonstration is in some respects more general and more direct, being deduced from the fundamental principles of the problem itself. We have made no suppositions, and the particular nature of the irreducible case has introduced no imaginary quantities.

Final solution on the new view. But the values of a and b still remain to be found from the preceding equations. And to this end I observe that the left-hand side of the equation

$$a^3 - b^3 + \frac{3}{2}(a^2 b - a b^2) = \frac{1}{2}\sqrt{-27 q^2 - 4 p^3}$$

can be made a perfect cube by adding the left-hand side of the equation

$$ab(a+b) = q,$$

multiplied by $\dfrac{3\sqrt{-3}}{2}$, and that the root of this cube is

$$\frac{1-\sqrt{-3}}{2}b - \frac{1+\sqrt{-3}}{2}a$$

so that, extracting the cube root of both sides, we shall have the expression

$$\frac{1-\sqrt{-3}}{2}b - \frac{1+\sqrt{-3}}{2}a$$

expressed in known quantities. And since the radical $\sqrt{-3}$ may also be taken negatively, we shall also have the expression

$$\frac{1+\sqrt{-3}}{2}b - \frac{1-\sqrt{-3}}{2}a$$

expressed in known quantities, from which the values of a and b can be deduced. And these values will contain the imaginary quantity $\sqrt{-3}$, which was introduced by multiplication, and will be reducible to the same form with the two roots

ON ALGEBRA. 87

$$m\sqrt[3]{A} + n\sqrt[3]{B} \text{ and } n\sqrt[3]{A} + m\sqrt[3]{B},$$

which we found above. The third root

$$c = -a - b$$

will then be expressed by $\sqrt[3]{A} + \sqrt[3]{B}$.

Office of imaginary quantities

By this method we see that the imaginary quantities employed have simply served to facilitate the extraction of the cube root without which we could not determine separately the values of a and b. And since it is apparently impossible to attain this object by a different method, we may regard it as a demonstrated truth' that the general expression of the roots of an equation of the third degree in the irreducible case cannot be rendered independent of imaginary quantities.

Let us now pass to *equations of the fourth degree*. We have already said that the artifice which was originally employed for resolving these equations consisted in so arranging them that the square root of the two sides could be extracted, by which they were reduced to equations of the second degree. The following is the procedure employed. Let

$$x^4 + px^2 + qx + r = 0$$

be the general equation of the fourth degree deprived of its second term, which can always be eliminated, as you know, by increasing or diminishing the roots by a suitable quantity. Let the equation be put in the form

$$x^4 = -px^2 - qx - r,$$

and to each side let there be added the terms $2x^2y + y^2$, which contain a new undetermined quantity y but which still leave the left-hand side of the equation a square. We shall then have

Biquadratic equations.

$$(x^2 + y)^2 = (2y - p)x^2 - qx + y^2 - r.$$

We must now make the right-hand side also a square. To this end it is necessary that

$$4(2y - p)(y^2 - r) = q^2,$$

in which case the square root of the right-hand side will have the form

$$x\sqrt{2y - p} - \frac{q}{2\sqrt{2y - p}}.$$

Supposing then that the quantity y satisfies the equation

$$4(2y - p)(y^2 - r) = q^2,$$

which developed becomes

$$y^3 - \frac{py^2}{2} - ry + \frac{pr}{2} - \frac{q^2}{8} = 0,$$

and which, as we see, is an equation of the third degree, the equation originally given may be reduced to the following by extracting the square root of its two members, viz.:

$$x^2 + y = x\sqrt{2y - p} - \frac{q}{2\sqrt{2y - p}},$$

where we may take either the plus or the positive value for the radical $\sqrt{2y - p}$, and shall consequently have two equations of the second degree to which the given equation has been reduced and the roots of which will give the four roots of the original equation.

ON ALGEBRA. 89

All of which furnishes us with our first instance of the decomposition of equations into others of lower degree.

The method of Descartes which is commonly followed in the elements of algebra is based upon the same principle and consists in assuming at the outset that the proposed equation is produced by the multiplication of two equations of the second degree, as

$$x^2 - ux + s = 0 \text{ and } x^2 + ux + t = 0,$$

The method of Descartes.

where u, s, and t are indeterminate coefficients. Multiplying them together we have

$$x^4 + (s + t - u^2)x + (s - t)ux + st = 0,$$

comparison of which with the original equation gives

$$s + t - u^2 = p, \ (s - t)u = q \text{ and } st = r.$$

The first two equations give

$$2s = p + u^2 + \frac{q}{u}, \ 2t = p + u^2 - \frac{q}{u}.$$

And if these values be substituted in the third equation of condition $st = r$, we shall have an equation of the sixth degree in u, which owing to its containing only even powers of u is resolvable by the rules for cubic equations. And if we substitute in this equation $2y - p$ for u^2, we shall obtain in y the same reduced equation that we found above by the old method.

Having the value of u^2 we have also the values of s and t, and our equation of the fourth degree will be decomposed into two equations of the second degree which will give the four roots sought. This method, as well as the preceding, has been the occasion of some hesitancy as to which of the three roots of the reduced cubic equation in u^2 or y should be employed.

The determined character of the roots

The difficulty has been well resolved in Clairaut's *Algebra*, where we are led to see directly that we always obtain the same four roots or values of x whatever root of the reduced equation we employ. But this generality is needless and prejudicial to the simplicity which is to be desired in the expression of the roots of the proposed equation, and we should prefer the formulæ which you have learned in the principal course and in which the three roots of the reduced equation are contained in exactly the same manner.

The following is another method of reaching the same formulæ, less direct than that which has already been expounded to you, but which, on the other hand has the advantage of being analogous to the method of Cardan for equations of the third degree.

I take up again the equation
$$x^4 + px^2 + qx + r = 0,$$
and I suppose
$$x = y + z + t.$$
Squaring I obtain
$$x^2 = y^2 + z^2 + t^2 + 2(yz + yt + zt).$$
Squaring again I have
$$x^4 = (y^2 + z^2 + t^2)^2 + 4(y^2 + z^2 + t^2)(yz + yt + zt) + 4(yz + yt + zt)^2;$$
but
$$(yz + yt + zt)^2 = y^2z^2 + y^2t^2 + z^2t^2 + 2y^2zt + 2yz^2t + 2yzt^2 = y^2z^2 + y^2t^2 + z^2t^2 + 2yzt(y + z + t).$$

ON ALGEBRA.

Substituting these three values of x, x^2, and x^4 in the original equation, and bringing together the terms multiplied by $y+z+t$ and the terms multiplied by $yz+yt+zt$, I have the transformed equation

A third method.

$$(y^2+z^2+t^2)^2+p(y^2+z^2+t^2)+$$
$$[4(y^2+z^2+t^2)+2p](yz+yt+zt)+$$
$$4(y^2z^2+y^2t^2+z^2t^2)+(8yzt+q)(y+z+t)+r=0.$$

We now proceed as we did with equations of the third degree, where we caused the terms containing $y+z$ to vanish, and in the same manner cause here the terms containing $y+z+t$ and $yz+yt+zt$ to disappear, which will give us the two equations of condition

$$8yzt+q=0 \text{ and } 4(y^2+z^2+t^2)+2p=0.$$

There remains the equation

$$(y^2+z^2+t^2)^2+p(y^2+z^2+t^2)+$$
$$4(y^2z^2+y^2t^2+z^2t^2)+r=0;$$

and the three together will determine the quantities y, z, and t. The second gives immediately

$$y^2+z^2+t^2=-\frac{p}{2},$$

which substituted in the third gives

$$y^2z^2+y^2t^2+z^2t^2=\frac{p^2}{16}-\frac{r}{4}.$$

The first, raised to its square, gives

$$y^2z^2t^2=\frac{q^2}{64}.$$

Hence, by the general theory of equations the three

quantities y^2, z^2, t^2 will be the roots of an equation of the third degree having the form

The reduced equation.

$$u^3 + \frac{p}{2} u^2 + \left(\frac{p^2}{16} - \frac{r}{4}\right) u - \frac{q^2}{64} = 0;$$

so that if the three roots of this equation, which we will call *the reduced equation*, be designated by a, b, c, we shall have

$$y = \sqrt{a}, \quad z = \sqrt{b}, \quad t = \sqrt{c},$$

and the value of x will be expressed by

$$\sqrt{a} + \sqrt{b} + \sqrt{c}.$$

Since the three radicals may each be taken with the plus sign or the minus sign, we should have, if all possible combinations were taken, eight different values for x. It is to be observed, however, that in the preceding analysis we employed the equation $y^2 z^2 t^2 = \frac{q^2}{64}$, whereas the equation immediately given is $yzt = -\frac{q}{8}$. Hence the product of the three quantities y, z, t, that is to say of the three radicals

$$\sqrt{a}, \sqrt{b}, \sqrt{c},$$

must have the contrary sign to that of the quantity q. Therefore, if q be a negative quantity, either three positive radicals or one positive and two negative radicals must be contained in the expression for x. And in this case we shall have the following four combinations only:

$$\sqrt{a} + \sqrt{b} + \sqrt{c}, \quad \sqrt{a} - \sqrt{b} - \sqrt{c},$$
$$-\sqrt{a} + \sqrt{b} - \sqrt{c}, \quad \sqrt{a} - \sqrt{b} + \sqrt{c},$$

which will be the four roots of the proposed equation of the fourth degree. But if q be a positive quantity, either three negative radicals or one negative and two positive radicals must be contained in the expression for x, which will give the following four other combinations as the roots of the proposed equation :*

Euler's formulæ.

$$-\sqrt{a}-\sqrt{b}-\sqrt{c},\ -\sqrt{a}+\sqrt{b}+\sqrt{c},$$
$$\sqrt{a}-\sqrt{b}+\sqrt{c},\ \sqrt{a}+\sqrt{b}-\sqrt{c}.$$

Now if the three roots a, b, c of the reduced equation of the third degree are all real and positive, it is evident that the four preceding roots will also all be real. But if among the three real roots a, b, c, any are negative, obviously the four roots of the given biquadratic equation will be imaginary. Hence, besides the condition for the reality of the three roots of the reduced equation it is also requisite in the first case, agreeably to the well-known rule of Descartes,

---

*These simple and elegant formulæ are due to Euler. But M. Bret, Professor of Mathematics at Grenoble, has made the important observation (see the *Correspondance sur l'Ecole Polytechnique*, t. II., 3me Cahier, p. 217) that they can give false values when imaginary quantities occur among the four roots.

In order to remove all difficulty and ambiguity we have only to substitute for one of these radicals its value as derived from the equation $\sqrt{a}\sqrt{b}\sqrt{c} = -\frac{q}{8}$. Then the formula

$$\sqrt{a}+\sqrt{b}-\frac{q}{8\sqrt{a}\sqrt{b}}$$

will give the four roots of the original equation by taking for a and b any two of the three roots of the reduced equation, and by taking the two radicals successively positive and negative.

The preceding remark should be added to article 777 of Euler's *Algebra* and to article 37 of the author's Note XIII of the *Traité de la résolution des équations numériques*.

Roots of a biquadratic equation.

that the coefficients of the terms of the reduced equation should be alternatively positive and negative, and consequently that p should be negative and $\frac{p^2}{16} - \frac{r}{4}$ positive, that is, $p^2 > 4r$. If one of these conditions is not realised the proposed biquadratic equation cannot have four real roots. If the reduced equation have but one real root, it will be observed, first, that by reason of its last term being negative the one real root of the equation must necessarily be positive. It is then easy to see from the general expressions which we gave for the roots of cubic equations deprived of their second term,—a form to which the reduced equation in u can easily be brought by simply increasing all the roots by the quantity $\frac{p}{6}$,—it is easy to see, I say, that the two imaginary roots of this equation will be of the form

$$f + g\sqrt{-1} \text{ and } f - g\sqrt{-1}.$$

Therefore, supposing a to be the real root and b, c the two imaginary roots, $\sqrt{a}$ will be a real quantity and $\sqrt{b} + \sqrt{c}$ will also be real for reasons which we have given above; while $\sqrt{b} - \sqrt{c}$ on the other hand will be imaginary. Whence it follows that of the four roots of the proposed biquadratic equation, the two first will be real and the two others will be imaginary.

As for the rest, if we make $u = s - \frac{p}{6}$ in the reduced equation in u, so as to eliminate the second term and to reduce it to the form which we have above examined, we shall have the following transformed equation in s:

$$s^3 - \left(\frac{p^2}{48} + \frac{r}{4}\right)s - \frac{p^3}{864} + \frac{pr}{24} - \frac{q^2}{64} = 0;$$

and the condition for the reality of the three roots of the reduced equation will be

$$4\left(\frac{p^2}{48} + \frac{r}{4}\right)^3 > 27\left(\frac{p^3}{864} - \frac{pr}{24} + \frac{q^2}{64}\right)^2.$$

LECTURE IV.

ON THE RESOLUTION OF NUMERICAL EQUATIONS.

Limits of the algebraical resolution of equations.

WE have seen how equations of the second, the third, and the fourth degree can be resolved. The fifth degree constitutes a sort of barrier to analysts, which by their greatest efforts they have never yet been able to surmount, and the general resolution of equations is one of the things that are still to be desired in algebra. I say in algebra, for if with the third degree the analytical expression of the roots is insufficient for determining in all cases their numerical value, *a fortiori* must it be so with equations of a higher degree; and so we find ourselves constantly under the necessity of having recourse to other means for determining numerically the roots of a given equation,—for to determine these roots is in the last resort the object of the solution of all problems which necessity or curiosity may offer.

I propose here to set forth the principal artifices which have been devised for accomplishing this important object. Let us consider any equation of the mth degree, represented by the formula

$$x^m + px^{m-1} + qx^{m-2} + rx^{m-3} + \ldots + u = 0,$$

in which x is the unknown quantity, p, q, r, ... the known positive or negative coefficients, and u the last term, not containing x and consequently also a known quantity. It is assumed that the values of these coefficients are given either in numbers or in lines; (it is indifferent which, seeing that by taking a given line as the unit or common measure of the rest we can assign to all the lines numerical values;) and it is clear that this assumption is always permissible when the equation is the result of a real and determinate problem. The problem set us is to find the value, or, if there be several, the values, of x which satisfy the equation, i. e. which render the sum of all its terms zero. Now any other value which may be given to x will render that sum equal to some positive or negative quantity, for since only integral powers of x enter the equation, it is plain that every real value of x will also give a real value for the quantity in question. The more that value approaches to zero, the more will the value of x which has produced it approach to a root of the equation. And if we find two values of x, of which one renders the sum of the terms equal to a positive quantity and the other to a negative quantity, we may be assured in advance that between these two values there will of necessity be at least one value which will render the expression zero and will consequently be a root of the equation.

Let P stand for the sum of all the terms of the

equation having the sign $+$ and Q for the sum of all the terms having the sign $-$; then the equation will be represented by

$$P - Q = 0.$$

Position of the roots of numerical equations. Let us suppose, for further simplicity, that the two values of x in question are positive, that A is the smaller, B the greater, and that the substitution of A for x gives a negative result and the substitution of B for x a positive result; i. e., that the value of $P-Q$ is negative when $x = A$, and positive when $x = B$.

Consequently, when $x = A$, P will be less than Q, and when $x = B$, P will be greater than Q. Now, from the very form of the quantities P and Q, which contain only positive terms and whole positive powers of x, it is clear that these quantities augment continuously as x augments, and that by making x augment by insensible degrees through all values from A to B, they also will augment by insensible degrees but in such wise that P will increase more than Q, seeing that from having been smaller than Q it will have become greater. Therefore, there must of necessity be some expression for the value of x between A and B which will make $P = Q$; just as two moving bodies which we suppose to be travelling along the same straight line and which having started simultaneously from two different points arrive simultaneously at two other points but in such wise that the body which was at first in the rear is now in advance of the other,—just as two such bodies, I say, must necessarily meet at some point in their path. That value of x, therefore, which will make $P = Q$ will be one of the roots of the equation, and such a value will lie of necessity between A and B.

The same reasoning may be employed for the other cases, and always with the same result.

Position of the roots of numerical equations.

The proposition in question is also demonstrable by a direct consideration of the equation itself, which may be regarded as made up of the product of the factors,

$$x-a,\ x-b,\ x-c,\ \ldots,$$

where $a, b, c, \ldots$ are the roots. For it is obvious that this product cannot, by the substitution of two different values for x, be made to change its sign, unless at least one of the factors changes its sign. And it is likewise easy to see that if more than one of the factors changes its sign, their number must be odd. Thus, if A and B are two values of x for which the factor $x-b$, for example, has opposite signs, then if A be larger than b, necessarily B must be smaller than b, or *vice versa*. Perforce, then, the root b will fall between the two quantities A and B.

As for imaginary roots, if there be any in the equation, since it has been demonstrated that they always occur in pairs and are of the form

$$f + g\sqrt{-1},\ f - g\sqrt{-1},$$

therefore if a and b are imaginary, the product of the factors $x-a$ and $x-b$ will be

$$(x-f-g\sqrt{-1})(x-f+g\sqrt{-1})=(x-f)^2+g^2,$$

a quantity which is always positive whatever value be given to x. From this it follows that alterations in the sign can be due only to real roots. But since the theorem respecting the form of imaginary roots cannot be rigorously demonstrated without employing the other theorem that every equation of an odd degree has necessarily one real root, a theorem of which the general demonstration itself depends on the proposition which we are concerned in proving, it follows that that demonstration must be regarded as a sort of vicious circle, and that it must be replaced by another which is unassailable.

Application of geometry to algebra. But there is a more general and simpler method of considering equations, which enjoys the advantage of affording direct demonstration to the eye of the principal properties of equations. It is founded upon a species of application of geometry to algebra which is the more deserving of exposition as it finds extended employment in all branches of mathematics.

Let us take up again the general equation proposed above and let us represent by straight lines all the successive values which are given to the unknown quantity x and let us do the same for the corresponding values which the left-hand side of the equation assumes in this manner. To this end, instead of supposing the right-hand side of the equation equal to zero, we suppose it equal to an undetermined quantity y. We lay off the values of x upon an indefinite straight line AB (Fig. 1), starting from a fixed point O at which x is zero and taking the positive values of x in the direction OB to the right of O and the negative values of x in the opposite direction to the left of O. Then let OP be any value of x. To represent the corresponding value of y we erect at P a perpendicular to the line OB and lay off on it the value of y in the direction PQ above the straight line OB if it is positive, and on the same perpendicular below OB if it is negative. We do the same for all the values of

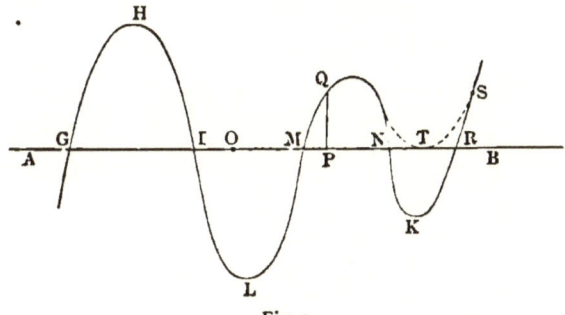

Fig. 1.

Representation of equations by curves.

x, positive as well as negative; that is, we lay off corresponding values of y upon perpendiculars to the straight line through all the points whose distance from the point O is equal to x. The extremities of all these perpendiculars will together form a straight line or a curve, which will furnish, so to speak, a picture of the equation

$$x^m + px^{m-1} + qx^{m-2} + \ldots + u = y.$$

The line AB is called the axis of the curve, O the origin of the abscissæ, $OP = x$ an abscissa, $PQ = y$ the corresponding ordinate, and the equations in x and y the equations of the curve. A curve such as that of Fig. 1 having been described in the manner indicated, it is clear that its intersections with the axis AB will give the roots of the proposed equation

Graphic resolution of equations.

$$x^m + p x^{m-1} + q x^{m-2} + \ldots + u = 0.$$

For seeing that this equation is realised only when in the equation of the curve y becomes zero, therefore those values of x which satisfy the equation in question and which are its roots can only be the abscissæ

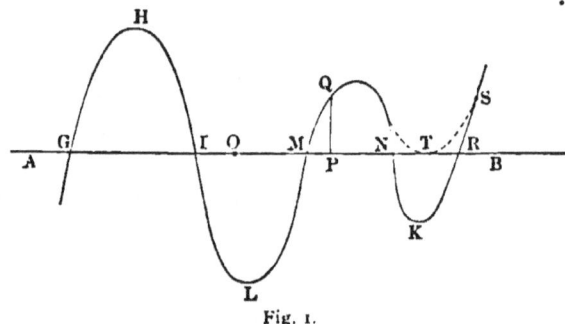

Fig. 1.

that correspond to the points at which the ordinates are zero, that is, to the points at which the curve cuts the axis AB. Thus, supposing the curve of the equation in x and y is that represented in Fig. 1, the roots of the proposed equation will be

OM, ON, OR, ... and $-OI$, $-OG$, ...

I give the sign — to the latter because the intersections I, G, ... fall on the other side of the point O. The consideration of the curve in question gives rise to the following general remarks upon equations:

RESOLUTION OF NUMERICAL EQUATIONS.   103

(1) Since the equation of the curve contains only whole and positive powers of the unknown quantity x it is clear that to every value of x there must correspond a determinate value of y, and that the value in question will be unique and finite so long as x is finite. But since there is nothing to limit the values of x they may be supposed infinitely great, positive as well as negative, and to them will correspond also values of y which are infinitely great. Whence it follows that the curve will have a continuous and single course, and that it may be extended to infinity on both sides of the origin O. *The consequences of the graphic resolution.*

(2) It also follows that the curve cannot pass from one side of the axis to the other without cutting it, and that it cannot return to the same side without having cut it twice. Consequently, between any two points of the curve on the same side of the axis there will necessarily be either no intersections or an even number of intersections; for example, between the points H and Q we find two intersections I and M, and between the points H and S we find four, I, M, N, R, and so on. Contrariwise, between a point on one side of the axis and a point on the other side, the curve will have an odd number of intersections; for example, between the points L and Q there is one intersection M, and between the points H and K there are three intersections, I, M, N, and so on.

For the same reason there can be no simple intersection unless on both sides of the point of intersection, above and below the axis, points of the curve are situated as are the points L, Q with respect to the intersection M. But two intersections, such as N and R, may approach each other so as ultimately to coincide at T. Then the branch QKS will take the form of the dotted line QTS and touch the axis at T, and will consequently lie in its whole extent above the axis; this is the case in which the two roots ON, OR are equal. If three intersections coincide at a point, —a coincidence which occurs when there are three equal roots,—then the curve will cut the axis in one additional point only, as in the case of a single point of intersection, and so on.

Consequently, if we have found for y two values having the same sign, we may be assured that between the two corresponding values of x there can fall only an even number of roots of the proposed equation; that is, that there will be none or there will be two, or there will be four, etc. On the other hand, if we have found for y two values having contrary signs, we may be assured that between the corresponding values of x there will necessarily fall an odd number of roots of the proposed equation; that is, there will be one, or there will be three, or there will be five, etc.; so that, in the case last mentioned, we may infer immediately that there will be at least one root of the proposed equation between the two values of x.

Conversely, every value of x which is a root of the equation will be found between some larger and some

Marginal note: Intersections indicate the roots.

smaller value of x which on being substituted for x in the equation will yield values of y with contrary signs.

This will not be the case, however, if the value of x is a double root; that is, if the equation contains two roots of the same value. On the other hand, if the value of x is a triple root, there will again exist a larger and a smaller value for x which will give to the corresponding values of y contrary signs, and so on with the rest. *Case of multiple roots.*

If, now, we consider the equation of the curve, it is plain in the first place, that by making $x=0$ we shall have $y=u$; and consequently that the sign of the ordinate y will be the same as that of the quantity u, the last term of the proposed equation. It is also easy to see that there can be given to x a positive or negative value sufficiently great to make the first term x^m of the equation exceed the sum of all the other terms which have the opposite sign to x^m; with the result that the corresponding value of y will have the same sign as the first term x^m. Now, if m is odd x^m will be positive or negative according as x is positive or negative, and if m is even, x^m will always be positive whether x be positive or not.

Whence we may conclude:

(1) That every equation of an odd degree of which the last term is negative has an odd number of roots between $x=0$ and some very large positive value of x, and an even number of roots between $x=0$ and some very large negative value of x, and consequently

that it has at least one real positive root. That, contrariwise, if the last term of the equation is positive it will have an odd number of roots between $x=0$ and some very large negative value of x, and an even number of roots between $x=0$ and some very large positive value of x, and consequently that it will have at least one real negative root.

General conclusions as to the character of the roots.

(2) That every equation of an even degree, of which the last term is negative, has an odd number of roots between $x=0$ and some very large positive value of x, as well as an odd number of roots between $x=0$ and some very large negative value of x, and consequently that it has at least one real positive root and one real negative root. That, on the other hand, if the last term is positive there will be an even number of roots between $x=0$ and some very large positive value of x, and also an even number of roots between $x=0$ and some very large negative value of x; with the result that in this case the equation may have no real root, whether positive or negative.

We have said that there could always be given to x a value sufficiently great to make the first term x^m of the equation exceed the sum of all the terms of contrary sign. Although this proposition is not in need of demonstration, seeing that, since the power x^m is higher than any of the other powers of x which enter the equation, it is bound, as x increases, to increase much more rapidly than these other powers; nevertheless, in order to leave no doubts in the mind, we shall offer a very simple demonstration of it,—a demonstration which will enjoy the collateral advantage of furnishing a limit beyond which we may be certain no root of the equation can be found.

To this end, let us first suppose that x is positive, and that k is the greatest of the coefficients of the negative terms. If we make $x = k+1$ we shall have
$$x^m = (k+1)^m = k(k+1)^{m-1} + (k+1)^{m-1}.$$
Similarly,
$$(k+1)^{m-1} = k(k+1)^{m-2} + (k+1)^{m-2},$$
$$(k+1)^{m-2} = k(k+1)^{m-3} + (k+1)^{m-3}$$
and so on; so that we shall finally have
$$(k+1)^m = k(k+1)^{m-1} + k(k+1)^{m-2} + k(k+1)^{m-3}$$
$$+ \ldots + k + 1.$$

Limits of the real roots of equations.

Now this quantity is evidently greater than the sum of all the negative terms of the equation taken positively, on the supposition that $x = k+1$. Therefore, the supposition $x = k+1$ necessarily renders the first term x^m greater than the sum of all the negative terms. Consequently, the value of y will have the same sign as x.

The same reasoning and the same result hold good when x is negative. We have here merely to change x into $-x$ in the proposed equation, in order to change the positive roots into negative roots, and *vice versa*.

In the same way it may be proved that if any value be given to x greater than $k+1$, the value of y will still have the same sign. From this and from what has been developed above, it follows immediately that the equation can have no root equal to or greater than $k+1$.

Limits of the positive and negative roots.

Therefore, in general, if k is the greatest of the coefficients of the negative terms of an equation, and if by changing the unknown quantity x into $-x$, h is the greatest of the coefficients of the negative terms of the new equation,—the first term always being supposed positive,—then all the real roots of the equation will necessarily be comprised between the limits $k+1$ and $-h-1$.

But if there are several positive terms in the equation preceding the first negative term, we may take for k a quantity less than the greatest negative coefficient. In fact it is easy to see that the formula given above can be put into the form
$$(k+1)^m = k(k+1)(k+1)^{m-2} + k(k+1)(k+1)^{m-3} + \ldots + (k+1)^2$$
and similarly into the following
$$(k+1)^m = k(k+1)^2(k+1)^{m-3} + k(k+1)^2(k+1)^{m-4} + \ldots + (k+1)^3$$
and so on.

Whence it is easy to infer that if $m-n$ is the exponent of the first negative term of the proposed equation of the mth degree, and if l is the largest coefficient of the negative terms, it will be sufficient if k is so determined that
$$k(k+1)^{n-1} = l.$$
And since we may take for k any larger value that we please, it will be sufficient to take

RESOLUTION OF NUMERICAL EQUATIONS. 109

$$k^n = l, \text{ or } k = \sqrt[n]{l}.$$

And the same will hold good for the quantity h as the limit of the negative roots.

If, now, the unknown quantity x be changed into $\frac{1}{z}$, the largest roots of the equation in x will be converted into the smallest in the new equation in z, and conversely. Having effected this transformation, and having so arranged the terms according to the powers of z that the first term of the equation is z^m, we may then in the same manner seek for the limits $K+1$ and $-H-1$ of the positive and negative roots of the equation in z. *Superior and inferior limits of the positive roots.*

Thus $K+1$ being larger than the largest value of z or of $\frac{1}{x}$, therefore, by the nature of fractions, $\frac{1}{K+1}$ will be smaller than the smallest value of x and similarly $\frac{1}{H+1}$ will be smaller than the smallest negative value of x.

Whence it may be inferred that all the positive real roots will necessarily be comprised between the limits

$$\frac{1}{K+1} \text{ and } k+1,$$

and that the negative real roots will fall between the limits

$$-\frac{1}{H+1} \text{ and } -h-1.$$

There are methods for finding still closer limits; but since they require considerable labor, the preceding method is, in the majority of cases, preferable, as being more simple and convenient.

<small>A further method for finding the limits.</small>
For example, if in the proposed equation $l+z$ be substituted for x, and if after having arranged the terms according to the powers of z, there be given to l a value such that the coefficients of all the terms become positive, it is plain that there will then be no positive value of z that can satisfy the equation. The equation will have negative roots only, and consequently l will be a quantity greater than the greatest value of x. Now it is easy to see that these coefficients will be expressed as follows:

$$p + ml,$$

$$q + (m-1)pl + \frac{m(m-1)}{2}l^2,$$

$$r + (m-2)ql + \frac{(m-1)(m-2)}{2}pl^2$$

$$+ \frac{m(m-1)(m-2)}{2.3}l^3,$$

and so on. Accordingly, it is only necessary to seek by trial the smallest value of l which will render them all positive.

But in the majority of cases it is not sufficient to know the limits of the roots of an equation; the thing necessary is to know the values of those roots, at least as approximately as the conditions of the problem require. For every problem leads in its last analysis to an equation which contains its solution; and if it is not in our power to resolve this equation, all

RESOLUTION OF NUMERICAL EQUATIONS. 111

the pains expended upon its formulation are a sheer loss. We may regard this point, therefore, as the most important in all analysis, and for this reason I have felt constrained to make it the principal subject of the present lecture. *The real problem, the finding of the roots.*

From the principles established above regarding the nature of the curve of which the ordinates y represent all the values which the left-hand side of an equation assumes, it follows that if we possessed some means of describing this curve we should obtain at once, by its intersections with the axis, all the roots of the proposed equation. But for this purpose it is not necessary to have all of the curve; it is sufficient to know the parts which lie immediately above and below each point of intersection. Now it is possible to find as many points of a curve as we please, and as near to one another as we please by successively substituting for x numbers which are very little different from one another, but which are still near enough for our purpose, and by taking for y the results of these substitutions in the left-hand side of the equation. If among the results of these substitutions two be found having contrary signs, we may be certain, by the principles established above, that there will be between these two values of x at least one real root. We can then by new substitutions bring these two limits still closer together and approach as nearly as we wish to the roots sought.

Calling the smaller of the two values of x which

have given results with contrary signs, A, and the larger B, and supposing that we wish to find the value of the root within a degree of exactness denoted by n, where n is a fraction of any degree of smallness we please, we proceed to substitute successively for x the following numbers in arithmetical progression :

Separation of the roots.

$$A+n,\ A+2n,\ A+3n,\ \ldots,$$

or

$$B-n,\ B-2n,\ B-3n,\ \ldots,$$

until a result is reached having the contrary sign to that obtained by the substitution of A or of B. Then one of the two successive values of x which have given results with contrary signs will necessarily be larger than the root sought, and the other smaller; and since by hypothesis these values differ from one another only by the quantity n, it follows that each of them approaches to within less than n of the root sought, and that the error is therefore less than n.

But how are the initial values substituted for x to be determined, so as on the one hand to avoid as many useless trials as possible, and on the other to make us confident that we have discovered by this method all the real roots of this equation. If we examine the curve of the equation it will be readily seen that the question resolves itself into so selecting the values of x that at least one of them shall fall between two adjacent intersections, which will be necessarily the case if the difference between two consecutive values is less than the smallest distance between two adjacent intersections.

Thus, supposing that D is a quantity smaller than the smallest distance between two intersections immediately following each other, we form the arithmetical progression

To find a quantity less than the difference between any two roots.

$$0, D, 2D, 3D, 4D, \ldots,$$

and we select from this progression only the terms which fall between the limits

$$\frac{1}{K+1} \text{ and } k+1,$$

as determined by the method already given. We obtain, in this manner, values which on being substituted for x ultimately give us all the positive roots of the equation, and at the same time give the initial limits of each root. In the same manner, for obtaining the negative roots we form the progression

$$0, -D, -2D, -3D, -4D, \ldots,$$

from which we also take only the terms comprised between the limits

$$-\frac{1}{H+1} \text{ and } -h-1.$$

Thus this difficulty is resolved. But it still remains to find the quantity D,—that is, a quantity smaller than the smallest interval between any two adjacent intersections of the curve with the axis. Since the abscissæ which correspond to the intersections are the roots of the proposed equation, it is clear that the question reduces itself to finding a quantity smaller than the smallest difference between two roots, neglecting the signs. We have, therefore, to seek, by the methods which were discussed in the lectures of the principal course, the equation whose roots are the differences between the roots of the proposed equation. And we must then seek, by the methods expounded above, a quantity smaller than the smallest root of this last equation, and take that quantity for the value of D.

The equation of differences. This method, as we see, leaves nothing to be desired as regards the rigorous solution of the problem, but it labors under great disadvantage in requiring extremely long calculations, especially if the proposed equation is at all high in degree. For example, if m is the degree of the original equation, that of the equation of differences will be $m(m-1)$, because each root can be subtracted from all the remaining roots, the number of which is $m-1$,—which gives $m(m-1)$ differences. But since each difference can be positive or negative, it follows that the equation of differences must have the same roots both in a positive and in a negative form; that consequently the equation must be wanting in all terms in which the unknown quantity is raised to an odd power; so that by taking the square of the differences as the unknown quantity, this unknown quantity can occur only in the $\frac{m(m-1)}{2}$th degree. For an equation of the mth degree, accordingly, there is requisite at the start a transformed

RESOLUTION OF NUMERICAL EQUATIONS. 115

equation of the $\frac{m(m-1)}{2}$th degree, which necessitates an enormous amount of tedious labor, if m is at all large. For example, for an equation of the 10th degree, the transformed equation would be of the 45th. And since in the majority of cases this disadvantage renders the method almost impracticable, it is of great importance to find a means of remedying it.

Impracticability of the method.

To this end let us resume the proposed equation of the mth degree,

$$x^m + p x^{m-1} + q x^{m-2} + \ldots + u = 0,$$

of which the roots are $a, b, c, \ldots$. We shall have then

$$a^m + p a^{m-1} + q a^{m-2} + \ldots + u = 0$$

and also

$$b^m + p b^{m-1} + q b^{m-2} + \ldots + u = 0.$$

Let $b - a = i$. Substitute this value of b in the second equation, and after developing the different powers of $a + i$ according to the well known binomial theorem, arrange the resulting equation according to the powers of i, beginning with the lowest. We shall have the transformed equation

$$P + Q i + R i^2 + \ldots + i^m = 0,$$

in which the coefficients $P, Q, R, \ldots$ have the following values

$$P = a^m + p a^{m-1} + q a^{m-2} + \ldots + u,$$
$$Q = m a^{m-1} + (m-1) p a^{m-2} + (m-2) q a^{m-3} + \ldots$$

Attempt to remedy the method.

$$R = \frac{m(m-1)}{2}a^{m-2} + \frac{(m-1)(m-2)}{2}pa^{m-3}$$
$$+ \frac{(m-2)(m-3)}{2}qa^{m-4} + \ldots$$

and so on. The law of formation of these expressions is evident.

Now, by the first equation in a we have $P=0$. Rejecting, therefore, the term P of the equation in i and dividing all the remaining terms by i, the equation in question will be reduced to the $(m-1)$th degree, and will have the form

$$Q + Ri + Si^2 + \ldots + i^{m-1} = 0.$$

This equation will have for its roots the $m-1$ differences between the root a and the remaining roots $b, c, \ldots$ Similarly, if b be substituted for a in the expressions for the coefficients $Q, R, \ldots$, we shall obtain an equation of which the roots are the difference between the root b and the remaining roots $a, c, \ldots$, and so on.

Accordingly, if a quantity can be found smaller than the smallest root of all these equations, it will possess the property required and may be taken for the quantity D, the value of which we are seeking.

If, by means of the equation $P=0$, a be eliminated from the equation in i, we shall get a new equation in i which will contain all the other equations of which we have just spoken, and of which it would only be necessary to seek the smallest root. But this new equation in i is nothing else than the equation of differences which we sought to dispense with.

In the above equation in i let us put it $i=\dfrac{1}{z}$. We shall have then the transformed equation in z,

Further improvement.

$$z^{m-1}+\frac{R}{Q}z^{m-2}+\frac{S}{Q}z^{m-3}+\ldots+\frac{1}{Q}=0,$$

and the greatest negative coefficient of this equation will, from what has been demonstrated above, give a value greater than its greatest root; so that calling L this greatest coefficient, $L+1$ will be a quantity greater than the greatest value of z. Consequently, $\dfrac{1}{L+1}$ will be a quantity smaller than the smallest positive value of i; and in like manner we shall find a quantity smaller than the smallest negative value of i. Accordingly, we may take for D the smallest of these two quantities, or some quantity smaller than either of them.

For a simpler result, and one which is independent of signs, we may reduce the question to finding a quantity L numerically greater than any of the coefficients of the equation in z, and it is clear that if we find a quantity N numerically smaller than the smallest value of Q and a quantity M numerically greater than the greatest value of any of the quantities R, S, ..., we may put $L=\dfrac{M}{N}$.

Let us begin with finding the values of M. It is not difficult to demonstrate, by the principles established above, that if $k+1$ is the limit of the positive

118   RESOLUTION OF NUMERICAL EQUATIONS.

Final resolution. roots and $-h-1$ the limit of the negative roots of the proposed equation, and if for a, $k+1$ and $-h-1$ be successively substituted in the expressions for R, $S, \ldots$, considering only the terms which have the same sign as the first,—it is easy to demonstrate that we shall obtain in this manner quantities which are greater than the greatest positive and negative values of $R, S, \ldots$ corresponding to the roots $a, b, c \ldots$ of the proposed equation; so that we may take for M the quantity which is numerically the greatest of these.

It accordingly only remains to find a value smaller than the smallest value of Q. Now it would seem that we could arrive at this in no other way than by employing the equation of which the different values of Q are the roots,—an equation which can only be reached by eliminating a from the following equations:

$$a^m + p a^{m-1} + q a^{m-2} + \ldots + u = 0,$$
$$m a^{m-1} + (m-1) p a^{m-2} + (m-2) q a^{m-3} + \ldots = Q.$$

It can be easily demonstrated by the theory of elimination that the resulting equation in Q will be of the mth degree, that is to say, of the same degree with the proposed equation; and it can also be demonstrated from the form of the roots of this equation that its next to the last term will be missing. If, accordingly, we seek by the method given above a quantity numerically smaller than the smallest root of this equation, the quantity found can be taken for N. The problem is therefore resolved by means of an equation of the same degree as the proposed equation.

The upshot of the whole is a follows,—where for the sake of simplicity I retain the letter x instead of the letter a. *Recapitulation.*

Let the following be the proposed equation of the mth degree:

$$x^m + px^{m-1} + qx^{m-2} + rx^{m-3} + \ldots = 0;$$

let k be the largest coefficient of the negative terms, and $m-n$ the exponent of x in the first negative term. Similarly, let h be the greatest coefficient of the terms having a contrary sign to the first term after x has been changed into $-x$; and let $m-n'$ be the exponent of x in the first term having a contrary sign to the first term of the equation as thus altered. Putting, then,

$$f = \sqrt[n]{k}+1 \quad \text{and} \quad g = \sqrt[n']{h}+1,$$

we shall have f and $-g$ for the limits of the positive and negative roots. These limits are then substituted successively for x in the following formulæ, neglecting the terms which have the same sign as the first term:

$$\frac{m(m-1)}{2}x^{m-2} + \frac{(m-1)(m-2)}{2}px^{m-3}$$
$$+ \frac{(m-2)(m-3)}{2}qx^{m-4} + \ldots,$$

$$\frac{m(m-1)(m-2)}{2.3}x^{m-3}$$
$$+ \frac{(m-1)(m-2)(m-3)}{2.3}px^{m-4} + \ldots,$$

and so on. Of these formulæ there will be $m-2$. Let the greatest of the numerical quantities obtained in this manner be called M. We then take the equation

The arithmetical progression revealing the roots.

$$m x^{m-1} + (m-1) p x^{m-2} + (m-2) q x^{m-3}$$
$$+ (m-3) r x^{m-4} + \ldots = y$$

and eliminate x from it by means of the proposed equation,—which gives an equation in y of the mth degree with its next to the last term wanting. Let V be the last term of this equation in y, and T the largest coefficient of the terms having the contrary sign to V, supposing y positive as well as negative. Then taking these two quantities T and V positive, N will be determined by the equation

$$\frac{N}{1-N} = \sqrt[n]{\frac{V}{T}}$$

where n is equal to the exponent of the last term having the contrary sign to V. We then take D equal to or smaller than the quantity $\frac{N}{M+N}$, and interpolate the arithmetical progression:

$$0, \ D, \ 2D, \ 3D, \ \ldots, \ -D, \ -2D, \ -3D, \ \ldots$$

between the limits f and $-g$. The terms of these progressions being successively substituted for x in the proposed equation will reveal all the real roots, positive as well as negative, by the changes of sign in the series of results produced by these substitutions, and they will at the same time give the first limits of these roots,—limits which can be narrowed as much as we please, as we already know.

If the last term V of the equation in y resulting from the elimination of x is zero, then N will be zero, and consequently D will be equal to zero. But in this case it is clear that the equation in y will have one root equal to zero and even two, because its next to the last term is wanting. Consequently the equation

Method of elimination

$$mx^{m-1} + (m-1)px^{m-2} + (m-2)qx^{m-3} + \ldots = 0.$$

will hold good at the same time with the proposed equation. These two equations will, accordingly, have a common divisor which can be found by the ordinary method, and this divisor, put equal to zero, will give one or several roots of the proposed equation, which roots will be double or multiple, as is easily apparent from the preceding theory; for if the last term Q of the equation in i is zero, it follows that

$$i = 0 \text{ and } a = b.$$

The equation in y is reduced, by the vanishing of its last term, to the $(m-2)$th degree,—being divisible by y^2. If after this division its last term should still be zero, this would be an indication that it had more than two roots equal to zero, and so on. In such a contingency we should divide it by y as many times as possible, and then take its last term for V, and the greatest coefficient of the terms of contrary sign to V for T, in order to obtain the value of D, which will enable us to find all the remaining roots of the proposed equation. If the proposed equation is of the third degree, as

$$x^3 + qx + r = 0,$$

we shall get for the equation in y,

$$y^3 + 3qy^2 - 4q^3 - 27r^2 = 0.$$

If the proposed equation is

$$x^4 + qx^2 + rx + s = 0$$

we shall obtain for the equation in y the following:

$$y^4 + 8ry^3 + (4q^3 - 16qs + 18r^2)y^2 + 256s^3 - 128s^2q^2$$
$$+ 16sq^4 + 144r^2sq - 4r^2q^3 - 27r^4 = 0$$

and so on.

General formulæ for elimination. Since, however, the finding of the equation in y by the ordinary methods of elimination may be fraught with considerable difficulty, I here give the general formulæ for the purpose, derived from the known properties of equations. We form, first, from the coefficients p, q, r of the proposed equation, the quantities x_1, x_2, x_3, ..., in the following manner:

$$x_1 = -p,$$
$$x_2 = -px_1 - 2q,$$
$$x_3 = -px_2 - qx_1 - 3r,$$
$$\ldots \ldots \ldots \ldots$$

We then substitute in the expressions for y, y^2, y^3, ... up to y^m, after the terms in x have been developed the quantities x_1 for x, x_2 for x^2, x_3 for x^3, and so forth, and designate by y_1, y_2, y_3, ... the values of y, y^2, y^3, ... resulting from these substitutions. We have then simply to form the quantities A, B, C from the formulæ

$$A = y_1,$$
$$B = \frac{Ay_1 - y_2}{2},$$
$$C = \frac{By_1 - Ay_2 + y_3}{3},$$
$$\ldots\ldots\ldots\ldots,$$

and we shall have the following equation in y:

$$y^m - Ay^{m-1} + By^{m-2} - Cy^{m-3} + \ldots = 0.$$

The value, or rather the limit of D, which we find by the method just expounded may often be much smaller than is necessary for finding all the roots, but there would be no further inconvenience in this than to increase the number of successive substitutions for x in the proposed equation. Furthermore, when there are as many results found as there are units in the highest exponent of the equation, we can continue these results as far as we wish by the simple addition of the first, second, third differences, etc., because the differences of the order corresponding to the degree of the equation are always constant.

General result.

We have seen above how the curve of the proposed equation can be constructed by successively giving different values to the abscissæ x and taking for the ordinates y the values resulting from these substitutions in the left-hand side of the equation. But these values for y can also be found by another very simple construction, which deserves to be brought to your notice. Let us represent the proposed equation by

$$a + bx + cx^2 + dx^3 + \ldots = 0$$

where the terms are taken in the inverse order. The equation of the curve will then be

$$y = a + bx + cx^2 + dx^3 + \ldots$$

A second construction for solving equations.

Drawing (Fig. 2) the straight line OX, which we take as the axis of abscissæ with O as origin, we lay off on this line the segment OI equal to the unit in terms of which we may suppose the quantities $a, b, c \ldots$, to be expressed; and we erect at the points OI the per-

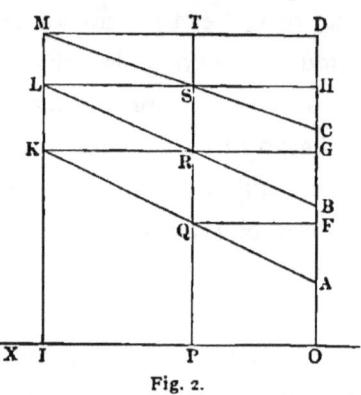

Fig. 2.

pendiculars OD, IM. We then lay off upon the line OD the segments

$$OA = a, \quad AB = b, \quad BC = c, \quad CD = d, \ldots,$$

and so on. Let $OP = x$, and at the point P let the perpendicular PT be erected. Suppose, for example, that d is the last of the coefficients $a, b, c, \ldots$, so that the proposed equation is only of the third degree, and that the problem is to find the value of

$$y = a + bx + cx^2 + dx^3.$$

The point D being the last of the points determined upon the perpendicular OD, and the point C the next

RESOLUTION OF NUMERICAL EQUATIONS. 125

to the last, we draw through D the line DM parallel to the axis OI, and through the point M where this line cuts the perpendicular IM we draw the straight line CM connecting M with C. Then through the point S where this last straight line cuts the perpendicular PT, we draw HSL parallel to OI, and through the point L where this parallel cuts the perpendicular IM we draw to the point B the straight line BL. Similarly, through the point R, where this last line cuts the perpendicular PT, we draw GRK parallel to OI, and through the point K, where this parallel cuts the perpendicular IM we draw to the first division point A of the perpendicular DO the straight line AK. The point Q where this straight line cuts the perpendicular PT will give the segment $PQ=y$.

The development and solution.

Through Q draw the line FQ parallel to the axis OP. The two similar triangles CDM and CHS give
$$DM(1): DC(d) = HS(x): CH(=dx).$$
Adding CB (c) we have
$$BH = c + dx.$$
Also the two similar triangles BHL and BGR give
$$HL(1): HB(c+dx) = GR(x): BG(=cx+dx^2).$$
Adding AB (b) we have
$$AG = b + cx + dx^2.$$
Finally the similar triangles AGK and AFQ give
$$GK(1): GA(b+cx+dx^2)$$
$$= FQ(x): FA(=bx+cx^2+dx^3);$$
and we obtain by adding OA (a)
$$OF = PQ = a + bx + cx^2 + dx^3 = y.$$

The same construction and the same demonstration hold, whatever be the number of terms in the proposed equation. When negative coefficients occur among a, b, c, ..., it is simply necessary to take them in the opposite direction to that of the positive coefficients. For example, if a were negative we should have to lay off the segment OA below the axis OI. Then we should start from the point A and add to it the segment $AB = b$. If b were positive, AB would be taken in the direction of OD; but if b were negative, AB would be taken in the opposite direction, and so on with the rest.

With regard to x, OP is taken in the direction of OI, which is supposed to be equal to positive unity, when x is positive; but in the opposite direction when x is negative.

A machine for solving equations. It would not be difficult to construct, on the foregoing model, an instrument which would be applicable to all values of the coefficients a, b, c, ..., and which by means of a number of movable and properly jointed rulers would give for every point P of the straight line OP the corresponding point Q, and which could be even made by a continuous movement to describe the curve. Such an instrument might be used for solving equations of all degrees; at least it could be used for finding the first approximate values of the roots, by means of which afterwards more exact values could be reached.

LECTURE V.

ON THE EMPLOYMENT OF CURVES IN THE SOLUTION OF PROBLEMS.

AS LONG as algebra and geometry travelled separate paths their advance was slow and their applications limited. But when these two sciences joined company, they drew from each other fresh vitality and thenceforward marched on at a rapid pace towards perfection. It is to Descartes that we owe the application of algebra to geometry,—an application which has furnished the key to the greatest discoveries in all branches of mathematics. The method which I last expounded to you for finding and demonstrating divers general properties of equations by considering the curves which represent them, is, properly speaking, a species of application of geometry to algebra, and since this method has extended applicacations, and is capable of readily solving problems whose direct solution would be extremely difficult or even impossible, I deem it proper to engage your attention in this lecture with a further view of this sub-

Geometry applied to algebra.

128 THE EMPLOYMENT OF CURVES.

ject,—especially since it is not ordinarily found in elementary works on algebra.

Method of resolution by curves. You have seen how an equation of any degree whatsoever can be resolved by means of a curve, of which the abscissæ represent the unknown quantity of the equation, and the ordinates the values which the left-hand member assumes for every value of the unknown quantity. It is clear that this method can be applied generally to all equations, whatever their form, and that it only requires them to be developed and arranged according to the different powers of the unknown quantity. It is simply necessary to bring all the terms of the equation to one side, so that the other side shall be equal to zero. Then taking the unknown quantity for the abscissa x, and the function of the unknown quantity, or the quantity compounded of that quantity and the known quantities, which forms one side of the equation, for the ordinate y, the curve described by these co-ordinates x and y will give by its intersections with the axis those values of x which are the required roots of the equation. And since most frequently it is not necessary to know all possible values of the unknown quantity but only such as solve the problem in hand, it will be sufficient to describe that portion of the curve which corresponds to these roots, thus saving much unnecessary calculation. We can even determine in this manner, from the shape of the curve itself, whether the problem has possible solutions satisfying the proposed conditions.

THE EMPLOYMENT OF CURVES. 129

Suppose, for instance, that it is required to find on the line joining two luminous points of given intensity, the point which receives a given quantity of light,— the law of physics being that the intensity of light decreases with the square of the distance. *Problem of the two lights.*

Let a be the distance between the two lights and x the distance between the point sought and one of the lights, the intensity of which at unit distance is M, the intensity of the other at that distance being N. The expressions $\dfrac{M}{x^2}$ and $\dfrac{N}{(a-x)^2}$, accordingly, give the intensity of the two lights at the point in question, so that, designating the total given effect by A, we have the equation

$$\frac{M}{x^2} + \frac{N}{(a-x)^2} = A$$

or

$$\frac{M}{x^2} + \frac{N}{(a-x)^2} - A = 0.$$

We will now consider the curve having the equation

$$\frac{M}{x^2} + \frac{N}{(a-x)^2} - A = y$$

in which it will be seen at once that by giving to x a very small value, positive or negative, the term $\dfrac{M}{x^2}$, while continuing positive, will grow very large, because a fraction increases in proportion as its denominator decreases, and it will be infinite when $x=0$. Further, if x be made to increase, the expression $\dfrac{M}{x^2}$ will constantly diminish; but the other expression

$\dfrac{N}{(a-x)^2}$, which was $\dfrac{N}{a^2}$ when $x=0$, will constantly increase until it becomes very large or infinite when x has a value very near to or equal to a.

Various solutions. Accordingly, if, by giving to x values from zero to a, the sum of these two expressions can be made to become less than the given quantity A, then the value of y, which at first was very large and positive, will become negative, and afterwards again become very large and positive. Consequently, the curve will cut the axis twice between the two lights, and the problem will have two solutions. These two solutions will be reduced to a single solution if the smallest value of

$$\frac{M}{x^2} + \frac{N}{(a-x)^2}$$

is exactly equal to A, and they will become imaginary if that value is greater than A, because then the value of y will always be positive from $x=0$ to $x=a$. Whence it is plain that if one of the conditions of the problem be that the required point shall fall between the two lights it is possible that the problem has no solution. But if the point be allowed to fall on the prolongation of the line joining the two lights, we shall see that the problem is always resolvable in two ways. In fact, supposing x negative, it is plain that the term $\dfrac{M}{x^2}$ will always remain positive and from being very large when x is near to zero, it will commence and keep decreasing as x increases until it grows very small or becomes zero when x is very great or infinite.

THE EMPLOYMENT OF CURVES.

The other term $\frac{N}{(a-x)^2}$, which at first was equal to $\frac{N}{a^2}$, also goes on diminishing until it becomes zero when x is negative infinity. It will be the same if x is positive and greater than a; for when $x=a$, the expression $\frac{N}{(a-x)^2}$ will be infinitely great; afterwards it will keep on decreasing until it becomes zero when x is infinite, while the other expression $\frac{M}{x^2}$ will first be equal to $\frac{M}{a^2}$ and will also go on diminishing towards zero as x increases.

Hence, whatever be the value of the quantity A, it is plain that the values of y will necessarily pass from positive to negative, both for x negative and for x positive and greater than a. Accordingly, there will be a negative value of x and a positive value of x greater than a which will resolve the problem in all cases. These values may be found by the general method by successively causing the values of x which give values of y with contrary signs, to approach nearer and nearer to each other. {General solution.}

With regard to the values of x which are less than a we have seen that the reality of these values depends on the smallest value of the quantity

$$\frac{M}{x^2} + \frac{N}{(a-x)^2}.$$

Directions for finding the smallest and greatest values of variable quantities are given in the Differential Calculus. We shall here content ourselves with remarking that the quantity in question will be a minimum when

Minimal values.
$$\frac{x}{a-x} = \sqrt[3]{\frac{M}{N}};$$

so that we shall have

$$x = \frac{a \sqrt[3]{M}}{\sqrt[3]{M} + \sqrt[3]{N}},$$

from which we get, as the smallest value of the expression

$$\frac{M}{x^2} + \frac{N}{(a-x)^2},$$

the quantity

$$\frac{(\sqrt[3]{M} + \sqrt[3]{N})^3}{a^2}.$$

Hence there will be two real values for x if this quantity is less than A; but these values will be imaginary if it is greater. The case of equality will give two equal values for x.

I have dwelt at considerable length on the analysis of this problem, (though in itself it is of slight importance,) for the reason that it can be made to serve as a type for all analogous cases.

The equation of the foregoing problem, having been freed from fractions, will assume the following form:

$$Ax^2(a-x)^2 - M(a-x)^2 - Nx^2 = 0.$$

With its terms developed and properly arranged it will be found to be of the fourth degree, and will consequently have four roots. Now by the analysis which we have just given, we can recognise at once the character of these roots. And since a method may spring from this consideration applicable to all equations of the fourth degree, we shall make a few brief remarks upon it in passing. Let the general equation be

Preceding analysis applied to biquadratic equations.

$$x^4 + px^2 + qx + r = 0.$$

We have already seen that if the last term of this equation be negative it will necessarily have two real roots, one positive and one negative; but that if the last term be positive we can in general infer nothing as to the character of its roots. If we give to this equation the following form

$$(x^2 - a^2)^2 + b(x+a)^2 + c(x-a)^2 = 0,$$

a form which developed becomes

$$x^4 + (b+c-2a^2)x^2 + 2a(b-c)x + a^4 + a^2(b+c) = 0,$$

and from this by comparison derive the following equations of condition

$$b+c-2a^2 = p, \quad 2a(b-c) = q, \quad a^4 + a^2(b+c) = r,$$

and from these, again, the following,

$$b+c = p+2a^2, \quad b-c = \frac{q}{2a}, \quad 3a^4 + pa^2 = r,$$

we shall obtain, by resolving the last equation,

$$a^2 = -\frac{p}{6} + \sqrt{\frac{r}{3} + \frac{p^2}{36}}.$$

If r be supposed positive, a^2 will be positive and real, and consequently a will be real, and therefore, also, b and c will be real.

Having determined in this manner the three quantities a, b, c, we obtain the transformed equation

$$(x^2 - a^2)^2 + b(x+a)^2 + c(x-a)^2 = 0.$$

Consideration of equations of the fourth degree.

Putting the right-hand side of this equation equal to y, and considering the curve having for abscissæ the different values of y, it is plain, that when b and c are positive quantities this curve will lie wholly above the axis and that consequently the equation will have no real root. Secondly, suppose that b is a negative quantity and c a positive quantity; then $x=a$ will give $y=4ba^2$,—a negative quantity. A very large positive or negative x will then give a very large positive y,—whence it is easy to conclude that the equation will have two real roots, one larger than a and one less than a. We shall likewise find that if b is positive and c is negative, the equation will have two real roots, one greater and one less than $-a$. Finally, if b and c are both negative, then y will become negative by making

$$x=a \text{ and } x=-a$$

and it will be positive and very large for a very large positive or negative value of x,—whence it follows that the equation will have two real roots, one greater than a and one less than $-a$. The preceding considerations might be greatly extended, but at present we must forego their pursuit.

It will be seen from the preceding example that the consideration of the curve does not require the equation to be freed from fractional expressions. The same may be said of radical expressions. There is an advantage even in retaining these expressions in the form given by the analysis of the problem; the advantage being that we may in this way restrict our attention to those signs of the radicals which answer to the special exigencies of each problem, instead of causing the fractions and the radicals to disappear and obtaining an equation arranged according to the different whole powers of the unknown quantity in which frequently roots are introduced which are entirely foreign to the question proposed. It is true that these roots are always part of the question viewed in its entire extent; but this wealth of algebraical analysis, although in itself and from a general point of view extremely valuable, may be inconvenient and burdensome in particular cases where the solution of which we are in need cannot by direct methods be found independently of all other possible solutions. When the equation which immediately flows from the conditions of the problem contains radicals which are essentially ambiguous in sign, the curve of that equation (constructed by making the side which is equal to zero, equal to the ordinate y) will necessarily have as many branches as there are possible different combinations of these signs, and for the complete solution it would be necessary to consider each of these branches. But this generality may be restricted by the particular conditions of the problem which determine the branch on which the solution is to be sought; the result being that we are spared much needless calculation,—an advantage which is not the least of those offered by

Advantages of the method of curves.

the method of solving equations from the consideration of curves.

<small>The curve of errors.</small>

But this method can be still further generalised and even rendered independent of the equation of the problem. It is sufficient in applying it to consider the conditions of the problem in and for themselves, to give to the unknown quantity different arbitrary values, and to determine by calculation or construction the errors which result from such suppositions according to the original conditions. Taking these errors as the ordinates y of a curve having for abscissæ the corresponding values of the unknown quantity, we obtain a continuous curve called *the curve of errors*, which by its intersections with the axis also gives all solutions of the problem. Thus, if two successive errors be found, one of which is an excess, and another a defect, that is, one positive and one negative, we may conclude at once that between these two corresponding values of the unknown quantity there will be one for which the error is zero, and to which we can approach as near as we please by successive substitutions, or by the mechanical description of the curve.

This mode of resolving questions by curves of errors is one of the most useful that have been devised. It is constantly employed in astronomy when direct solutions are difficult or impossible. It can be employed for resolving important problems of geometry and mechanics and even of physics. It is properly

THE EMPLOYMENT OF CURVES.

speaking the *regula falsi*, taken in its most general sense and rendered applicable to all questions where there is an unknown quantity to be determined. It can also be applied to problems that depend on two or several unknown quantities by successively giving to these unknown quantities different arbitrary values and calculating the errors which result therefrom, afterwards linking them together by different curves, or reducing them to tables; the result being that we may by this method obtain directly the solution sought

Solution of a problem by the curve of errors.

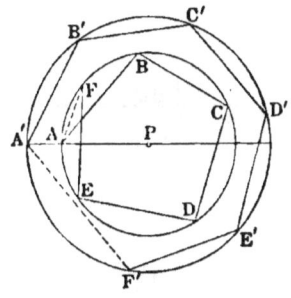

Fig. 3.

without preliminary elimination of the unknown quantities.

We shall illustrate its use by a few examples.

Required a circle in which a polygon of given sides can be inscribed.

This problem gives an equation which is proportionate in degree to the number of sides of the polygon. To solve it by the method just expounded we describe any circle $ABCD$ (Fig. 3) and lay off in this circle the given sides AB, BC, CD, DE, EF of the

138   THE EMPLOYMENT OF CURVES.

Problem of the circle and inscribed polygon.
polygon, which for the sake of simplicity I here suppose to be pentagonal. If the extremity of the last side falls on A, the problem is solved. But since it is very improbable that this should happen at the first trial we lay off on the straight line PR (Fig. 4) the radius PA of the circle, and erect on it at the point A the perpendicular AF equal to the chord AF of the arc AF which represents the error in the supposition made regarding the length of the radius PA. Since this error is an excess, it will be necessary to describe

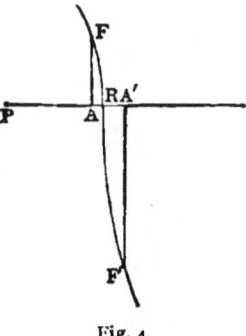

Fig. 4.

a circle having a larger radius and to perform the same operation as before, and so on, trying circles of various sizes. Thus, the circle having the radius PA gives the error $F'A'$ which, since it falls on the hither side of the point A', should be accounted negative. It will consequently be necessary in Fig. 4 in applying the ordinate $A'F'$ to the abscissa PA' to draw that ordinate below the axis. In this manner we shall obtain several points F, F', ..., which will lie on a curve of which the intersection R with the axis PA

will give the true radius *PR* of the circle satisfying
the problem, and we shall find this intersection by
successively causing the points of the curve lying on
the two sides of the axis as F, F' . . . to approach
nearer and nearer to one another.

Solution of a second problem by the curve of errors.

*From a point, the position of which is unknown, three
objects are observed, the distances of which from one another are known. The three angles formed by the rays of
light from these three objects to the eye of the observer are
also known. Required the position of the observer with
respect to the three objects.*

If the three objects be joined by three straight
lines, it is plain that these three lines will form with
the visual rays from the eye of the observer a triangular pyramid of which the base and the three face angles forming the solid angle at the vertex are given.
And since the observer is supposed to be stationed at
the vertex, the question is accordingly reduced to determining the dimensions of this pyramid.

Since the position of a point in space is completely
determined by its three distances from three given
points, it is clear that the problem will be resolved, if
the distances of the point at which the observer is
stationed from each of the three objects can be determined. Taking these three distances as the unknown
quantities we shall have three equations of the second
degree. which after elimination will give a resultant
equation of the eighth degree; but taking only one of
these distances and the relations of the two others to it

for the unknown quantities, the final equation will be only of the fourth degree. We can accordingly rigorously solve this problem by the known methods; but the direct solution, which is complicated and inconvenient in practice, may be replaced by the following which is reached by the curve of errors.

Problem of the observer and three objects

Let the three successive angles APB, BPC, CPD (Fig. 5) be constructed, having the vertex P and respectively equal to the angles observed between the first object and the second, the second and the third,

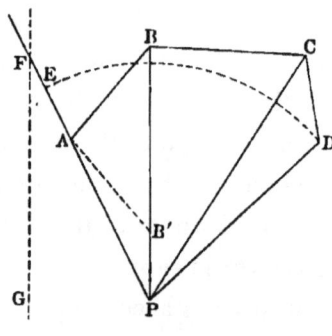

Fig. 5.

the third and the first; and let the straight line PA be taken at random to represent the distance from the observer to the first object. Since the distance of that object to the second is supposed to be known, let it be denoted by AB, and let it be laid off on the line AB. We shall in this way obtain the distance BP of the second object to the observer. In like manner, let BC, the distance of the second object to the third, be laid off on BC, and we shall have the distance PC of that object to the observer. If, now, the

THE EMPLOYMENT OF CURVES. 141

distance of the third object to the first be laid off on the line CD, we shall obtain PD as the distance of the first object to the observer. Consequently, if the distance first assumed is exact, the two lines PA and PD will necessarily coincide. Making, therefore, on the line PA, prolonged if necessary, the segment $PE = PD$, if the point E does not fall upon the point A, the difference will be the error of the first assumption PA. Having drawn the straight line PR (Fig. 6) we lay off upon it from the fixed point P, the abscissa PA, and apply to it at right angles the ordinate EA; we shall have the point E of the curve of errors ERS.

Employment of the curve of errors.

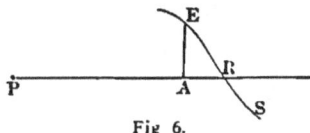

Fig. 6.

Taking other distances for PA, and making the same construction, we shall obtain other errors which can be similarly applied to the line PR, and which will give other points in the same curve.

We can thus trace this curve through several points, and the point R where it cuts the axis PR will give the distance PR, of which the error is zero, and which will consequently represent the exact distance of the observer from the first object. This distance being known, the others may be obtained by the same construction.

It is well to remark that the construction we have been considering gives for each point A of the line

PA, two points *B* and *B'* of the line *PB*; for, since the distance *AB* is given, to find the point *B* it is only necessary to describe from the point *A* as centre and with radius *AB* an arc of a circle cutting the straight line *PB* at the two points *B* and *B'*,—both of which points satisfy the conditions of the problem. In the same manner, each of these last-mentioned points will give two more upon the straight line *PC*, and each of the last will give two more on the straight line *PD*. Whence it follows that every point *A* taken upon the straight line *PA* will in general give eight upon the straight line *PD*, all of which must be separately and successively considered to obtain all the possible solutions. I have said, *in general*, because it is possible (1) for the two points *B* and *B'* to coincide at a single point, which will happen when the circle described with the centre *A* and radius *AB* touches the straight line *PB*; and (2) that the circle may not cut the straight line *PB* at all, in which case the rest of the construction is impossible, and the same is also to be said regarding the points *C*, *D*. Accordingly, drawing the line *GF* parallel to *BP* and at a distance from it equal to the given line *AB*, the point *F* at which this line cuts the line *PE*, prolonged if necessary, will be the limit beyond which the points *A* must not be taken if we desire to obtain possible solutions. There exist also limits for the points *B* and *C*, which may be employed in restricting the primitive suppositions made with respect to the distance *PA*.

<small>Eight possible solutions of the preceding problem.</small>

The eight points D, which depend in general on each point A, answer to the eight solutions of which the problem is susceptible, and when one has no special datum by means of which it can be determined which of these solutions answer best to the case proposed, it is indispensable to ascertain them all by employing for each one of the eight combinations a special curve of errors. But if it be known, for example, that the distance of the observer to the second object is greater or less than his distance to the first, it will then be necessary to take on the line PB only the point B in the first case and the point B' in the second,—a course which will reduce the eight combinations one-half. If we had the same datum with regard to the third object relatively to the second, and with regard to the first object relatively to the third, then the points C and D would be determined, and we should have but a single solution.

Reduction of the possible solutions in practice.

These two examples may suffice to illustrate the uses to which the method of curves can be put in solving problems. But this method, which we have presented, so to speak, in a mechanical manner, can also be submitted to analysis.

The entire question in fact is reducible to the description of a curve which shall pass through a certain number of points, whether these points be given by calculation or construction, or whether they be given by observation or single experiences entirely independent of one another. The problem is in truth in-

General conclusion on the method of curves.

determinate, for strictly speaking there can be made to pass through a given number of points an infinite number of different curves, regular or irregular, that is, subject to equations or arbitrarily drawn by the hand. But the question is not to find any solutions whatever but the simplest and easiest in practice.

Thus if there are only two points given, the simplest solution is a straight line between the two points. If there are three points given, the arc of a circle is drawn through these points, for the arc of a circle after the straight line is the simplest line that can be described.

But if the circle is the simplest curve with respect to description, it is not so with respect to the equation between its abscissæ and rectangular ordinates. In this latter point of view, those curves may be regarded as the simplest of which the ordinates are expressed by an integral rational function of the abscissæ, as in the following equation

$$y = a + bx + cx^2 + dx^3 + \ldots,$$

where y is the ordinate and x the abscissa. Curves of this class are called in general *parabolic*, because they may be regarded as a generalisation of the parabola,—a curve represented by the foregoing equation when it has only the first three terms. We have already illustrated their employment in resolving equations, and their consideration is always useful in the approximate description of curves, for the reason that a curve of this kind can always be made to pass

THE EMPLOYMENT OF CURVES. 145

through as many points of a given curve as we please, —it being only necessary to take as many undetermined coefficients a, b, c, ... as there are points given, and to determine these coefficients so as to obtain the abscissæ and ordinates for these points. Now it is clear that whatever be the curve proposed, the parabolic curve so described will always differ from it by less and less according as the number of the different points is larger and larger and their distance from one another smaller and smaller.

<small>Parabolic curves.</small>

Newton was the first to propose this problem. The following is the solution which he gave of it:

Let P, Q, R, S, ... be the values of the ordinates y corresponding to the values p, q, r, s, ... of the abscissæ x; we shall have the following equations

$$P = a + bp + cp^2 + dp^3 + \ldots,$$
$$Q = a + bq + cq^2 + dq^3 + \ldots,$$
$$R = a + br + cr^2 + dr^3 + \ldots,$$
$$\cdot \quad \cdot \cdot \quad \cdot \cdot$$

The number of these equations must be equal to the number of the undetermined coefficients a, b, c, ... Subtracting these equations from one another, the remainders will be divisible by $q-p$, $r-q$, ..., and we shall have after such division

$$\frac{Q-P}{q-p} = b + c(q+p) + d(q^2 + qp + p^2) + \ldots,$$
$$\frac{R-Q}{r-q} = b + c(r+q) + d(r^2 + rq + q^2) + \ldots,$$

Let

$$\frac{Q-P}{q-p} = Q_1, \quad \frac{R-Q}{r-q} = R_1, \quad \frac{S-R}{s-r} = S_1, \ldots$$

Newton's problem. We shall find in like manner, by subtraction and division, the following:

$$\frac{R_1 - Q_1}{r-p} = c + d(r+q+p) + \ldots,$$

$$\frac{S_1 - R_1}{s-q} = c + d(s+r+q) + \ldots,$$

Further let

$$\frac{R_1 - Q_1}{r-p} = R_2, \quad \frac{S_1 - R_1}{s-q} = S_2, \ldots$$

We shall have

$$\frac{S_2 - R_2}{s-p} = d + \ldots,$$

and so on.

In this manner we shall find the value of the coefficients a, b, c, ... commencing with the last; and, substituting them in the general equation

$$y = a + bx + cx^2 + dx^3 + \ldots,$$

we shall obtain, after the appropriate reductions have been made, the formula

$$\begin{aligned} y = P &+ Q_1(x-p) + R_2(x-p)(x-q) \\ &+ S_3(x-p)(x-q)(x-r) + \ldots, \end{aligned} \quad \ldots (1)$$

which can be carried as far as we please.

But this solution may be simplified by the following consideration.

Since y necessarily becomes P, Q, R ..., when x

THE EMPLOYMENT OF CURVES. 147

becomes p, q, r, it is easy to see that the expression for y will be of the form

$$y = AP + BQ + CR + DS + \ldots \ldots \quad (2)$$

Simplification of Newton's solution.

where the quantities $A, B, C, \ldots$ are so expressed in terms of x that by making $x = p$ we shall have

$$A = 1, \ B = 0, \ C = 0, \ \ldots,$$

and by making $x = q$ we shall have

$$A = 0, \ B = 1, \ C = 0, \ D = 0, \ \ldots,$$

and by making $x = r$ we shall similarly have

$$A = 0, \ B = 0, \ C = 1, \ D = 0, \ \ldots \text{ etc.}$$

Whence it is easy to conclude that the values of $A, B, C, \ldots$ must be of the form

$$A = \frac{(x-q)(x-r)(x-s)\ldots}{(p-q)(p-r)(p-s)\ldots},$$

$$B = \frac{(x-p)(x-r)(x-s)\ldots}{(q-p)(q-r)(q-s)\ldots},$$

$$C = \frac{(x-p)(x-q)(x-s)\ldots}{(r-p)(r-q)(r-s)\ldots},$$

where there are as many factors in the numerators and denominators as there are points given of the curve less one.

The last expression for y (see equation 2), although different in form, is the same as equation 1. To show this, the values of the quantities $Q_1, R_2, S_3, \ldots$ need only be developed and substituted in equation 1 and the terms arranged with respect to the quantities $P, Q, R, \ldots$ But the last expression for y (equation 2) is preferable, partly because of the simplicity of the

148   THE EMPLOYMENT OF CURVES.

<small>Possible uses of Newton's problem.</small>

analysis from which it is derived, and also because of its form, which is more convenient for computation.

Now, by means of this formula, which it is not difficult to reduce to a geometrical construction, we are able to find the value of the ordinate y for any abscissa x, because the ordinates P, Q, R, ... for the given abscissæ p, q, r, ... are known. Thus, if we have several of the terms of any series, we can find any intermediate term that we wish,—an expedient which is extremely valuable for supplying lacunæ which may arise in a series of observations or experiments, or in tables calculated by formulæ or in given constructions.

If this theory now be applied to the two examples discussed above and to similar examples in which we have errors corresponding to different suppositions, we can directly find the error y which corresponds to any intermediate supposition x by taking the quantities P, Q, R, ..., for the errors found, and p, q, r, ... for the suppositions from which they result. But since in these examples the question is to find not the error which corresponds to a given supposition, but the supposition for which the error is zero, it is clear that the present question is the opposite of the preceding and that it can also be resolved by the same formula by reciprocally taking the quantities p, q, r, ... for the errors, and the quantities P, Q, R, ... for the corresponding suppositions. Then x will be the error for the supposition y; and consequently, by making

$x=0$, the value of y will be that of the supposition for which the error is zero.

Let $P, Q, R, \ldots$ be the values of the unknown quantity in the different suppositions, and $p, q, r \ldots$ the errors resulting from these suppositions, to which the appropriate signs are given. We shall then have for the value of the unknown quantity of which the error is zero, the expression

Application of Newton's problem to the preceding examples.

$$AP + BQ + CR + \ldots,$$

in which the values of $A, B, C \ldots$ are

$$A = \frac{q}{q-p} \times \frac{r}{r-p} \times \cdots,$$

$$B = \frac{p}{p-q} \times \frac{r}{r-q} \times \cdots,$$

$$C = \frac{p}{p-r} \times \frac{q}{q-r} \times \cdots,$$

where as many factors are taken as there are suppositions less one.

APPENDIX.

NOTE ON THE ORIGIN OF ALGEBRA.

THE impression (p. 54) that Diophantus was the "inventor" of algebra, which sprang, in its Diophantine form, full-fledged from his brain, was a widespread one in the eighteenth and in the beginning of the nineteenth century. But, apart from the intrinsic improbability of this view which is at variance with the truth that science is nearly always gradual and organic in growth, modern historical researches have traced the germs and beginnings of algebra to a much remoter date, even in the line of European historical continuity. The Egyptian book of Ahmes contains examples of equations of the first degree. The early Greek mathematicians performed the partial resolution of equations of the second and third degree by geometrical methods. According to Tannery, an embryonic indeterminate analysis existed in Pre-Christian times (Archimedes, Hero, Hypsicles). But the merit of Diophantus as organiser and inaugurator of a more systematic short-hand notation, at least in the European line, remains; he enriched whatever was handed down to him with the most manifold extensions and applications, betokening his originality and genius, and carried the science of algebra to its highest pitch of perfection among the Greeks. (See Cantor, *Geschichte der Mathematik*, second edition, Vol. I., p. 438, et seq.; Ball, *Short Account of the History of Mathematics*, second edition, p. 104 et seq.; Fink, *A Brief History of Mathematics*, pp. 63 et seq., 77 et seq. (Chicago: The Open Court Publishing Co.)

The development of Hindu algebra is also to be noted in connexion with the text of pp. 59-60. The Arabs, who had considerable commerce with India, drew not a little of their early knowledge from the works of the Hindus. Their algebra rested on both that of the Hindus and the Greeks. (See Ball, *op. cit.*, p. 150 et seq.; Cantor, *op. cit.*, Vol. I., p. 651 et seq.).—*Trans.*

INDEX.

Academies, rise of, 62, 63.
Ahmes, 151.
Algebra, definition of, 2; history of, 54 et seq., 151; essence of, 55; the name of, 59; among the Arabs, 59 et seq., 152; in Europe, 60; in Italy, 64; in India, 152; the generality of, 69; hand-writing of, 69; application of geometry to, 100 et seq., 127 et seq.
Algebraical resolution of equations, limits of the, 96.
Alligation, generally, 44 et seq.; alternate, 47.
Analysis, indeterminate, 47 et seq., 55.
Angle, trisection of an, 62, 81.
Angular sections, theory of, 80.
Annuities, 16.
Apollonius, 54, 59.
Arabs, Algebra among the, 59 et seq., 152.
Archimedes, 54, 58 footnote, 151.
Arithmetic, universal, 2 et seq.; operations of, 24 et seq.
Arithmetical progression revealing the roots, 112 et seq., 120.
Arithmetical proportion, 12.
Astronomy, mechanics, and physics, curves of errors in, 136.
Average life, 45 et seq.

Bachet de Méziriac, 58.
Ball, 152.
Binomial theorem, 115.
Binomials, extraction of the square roots of two imaginary, 77.
Biquadratic equations, 63, 88, 94, 133.

Bombelli, 63, 64.
Bret, M., 93 footnote.
Briggs, 20.
Buteo, 61.

Cantor, 54 footnote; 60, footnote, 152.
Cardan, 60, 61, 68, 82, 90.
Checks on multiplication and division, 39.
Circle, 144; squaring of the, 62; and inscribed polygon, problem of the, 138.
Clairaut, 69, 90.
Coefficients, indeterminate, 89; greatest negative, 107 et seq., 117.
Common divisor of two equations, 121.
Complements, subtraction by, 26.
Constantinople, 58.
Continued fractions, solution of alligation by, 50 et seq.
Convergents, 7.
Cube, duplication of the, 62.
Cube roots of a quantity, the three, 70.
Cubic radicals, 75.
Curves, representation of equations by, 101 et seq; employment of in the solution of problems, 127-149; method of, submitted to analysis, 143 et seq.; advantages of the method of, 135, 144.

Decimal, fractions, 9; numbers, 27 et seq.
Decimals, multiplication of, 30; division of, 31.

DeMorgan, v.
Descartes, viii, 60, 65, 89, 93, 127.
Differences, the equation of, 114 et seq., 123.
Differential Calculus, 131.
Diophantine problems, 55.
Diophantus, 54 et seq, 151.
Division, by *nine*, 34; by *eight*, 34; by *seven*, 34 et seq.; of decimals, 31.
Divisor, greatest common, 2 et seq.
Dühring, E. v.
Duodecimal system, 32.

Ecole Normale, v, xi, 12.
Economy of thought, vii.
Efflux, law of, 42.
Eleven, the number, test of divisibility by, 37.
Elimination, method of, 121; general formulæ for, 122.
Equations, of the second degree, 56; of the third degree, 60, 66, 82; of the fourth degree, 63, 87, 133; of the fifth degree, 64; theory of, 65, 84; biquadratic, 88; limits of the algebraical resolution of, 96; of the fifth degree, 96; of the mth degree. 96; general remarks upon the roots of, 102 et seq.; graphic resolution of, 102; of an odd degree, roots of, 105; of an even degree, roots of, 106; real roots of, limits of the, 107 et seq.; common divisor of two, 121; constructions for solving, 100 et seq., 124; a machine for solving, 126.
Equi-different numbers, 13.
Errors, curve of, 136 et seq.
Euclid, 2, 57.
Euler, viii, x, 93.
Europe, algebra in 60.
Evolution, 11, 40.
Experiments, average of, 46; an expedient for supplying lacunæ in a series of, 148.

Falling stone, spaces traversed by a, 42.
False, rule of, 137.
Fermat, 58.
Ferrari, Louis, 64.

Ferreus, Scipio, 60 et seq.
Fifth degree, equations of the, 96.
Fink, 152.
Fourth degree, equations of the, 133.
Fractional expressions in equations, 134.
Fractions, 2 et seq.; continued, 3 et seq.; converging, 6; decimal, 9; origin of continued, 10.
France, 58, 61.

Galileo, ix.
Geometers, ancient, 54 et seq., 58, 59.
Geometrical, proportion, 13; calculus, 24.
Geometry, 24, 60; application of to algebra, 100 et seq., 127 et seq.
Germany, 61.
Girard, Albert, 62.
Grain, of different prices, 44.
Greeks, mathematics of the, vii, 54 et seq., 151.

Hand-writing of algebra, 69.
Harriot, 65.
Hero, 59, 151.
Horses, 43.
Hudde, 65, 82.
Huygens, ix, 10.
Hypsicles, 151.

Imaginary binomials, square roots of, 77.
Imaginary expressions, 79 et seq., 83.
Imaginary quantities, office of the, 87.
Imaginary roots, occur in pairs, 99.
Indeterminate analysis, 47 et seq., 55.
Indeterminate coefficients, 89.
Indeterminates, the method of, 83.
Ingredients, 48.
Interest, 15,
Intersections, with the axis give roots, 102 et seq, 113.
Inventors, great, 22.
Involution and evolution. 11.
Irreducible case, 61, 65, 69, 73, 82.
Italy, cradle of algebra in Europe, 61, 64.

Laborers, work of, 41.
Lagrange, J. L., v, vii et seq.

INDEX. 155

Laplace, v, xi.
Lavoisier, xii.
Leibnitz, viii.
Life insurance, 45 et seq
Life, probability of, 46.
Light, law of the intensity of, 129.
Lights, problem of the two, 129 et seq.
Limits of roots, 107–120.
Logarithms, 16 et seq., 40; advantages in calculating by, 28; origin of, 19; tables of, 20.

Machine for solving equations, 124–126.
Mathematics, wings of, 24; exactness of, 43; evolution of, vii.
Mean values, 45 et seq.
Mechanics, astronomy, and physics, curves of errors in, 136.
Metals, mingling of, by fusion, 44.
Méziriac, Bachet de, 58.
Minimal values, 132.
Mixtures, rule of, 44 et seq., 49.
Monge, v, xi.
Mortality, tables of, 45.
Moving bodies, two, 98.
Multiple roots, 105.
Multiplication, abridged methods of, 26 et seq.; inverted, 28; approximate, 29; of decimals, 30.
Music, 22.

Napier, 17 et seq.
Napoleon, xii.
Negative roots, 60.
Newton, his problem, 145; viii.
Nine, property of the number, 31 et seq.; property of the number generalised, 33.
Nizze, 58 footnote.
Numeration, systems of, 1.
Numerical equations, resolution of, 96–126; conditions of the resolution of, 97; position of the roots of, 98. See *Equations.*

Observations, expedient for supplying lacunæ in series of, 148.
Observer, problem of the, and three objects, 140.
Oughtred, 30.

Paciolus, Lucas, 59, 60.
Pappus, 59.
Parabolic curves, 144 et seq.
Peletier, 61.
Peyrard, 58.
Physics, astronomy, and mechanics, curves of errors in, 136.
Planetarium, 9.
Point in space, position of a, 139.
Polygon, problem of the circle and inscribed, 138.
Polytechnic School, v. xi.
Positive roots, superior and inferior limits of the, 109.
Powers, 10 et seq.
Practice, theory and, 43.
Present value, 15.
Printing, invention of, 59.
Probabilities, calculus of, 45 et seq.
Problems, 110; for solution, 62; employment of curves in the solution of, 127–149.
Proclus, 59.
Progressions, theory of, 12, 14.
Proportion, 11 et seq.
Ptolemy, 59.

Radical expressions in equations, 134
Radicals, cubic, 75.
Ratios, constant, 42; 2, 11 et seq.
Reality of roots, 76, 83, 85, 93.
Regula falsi, 137, 148.
Remainders, theory of, 34 et seq., 38.
   negative, 35 et seq.
Romans, mathematics of the, 54.
Roots, negative, 60; of equations of the third degree, 71; the reality of the, 71, 76, 79, 83, 85, 93; of a biquadratic equation, 94; multiple, 105; superior and inferior limits of the positive, 109; method for finding the limits of, 110; separation of the, 112; the arithmetical progression revealing the, 112 et seq., 120; quantity less than the difference between any two, 113; smallest, 116 et seq.; limits of the positive and negative, 119.
Rule, Cardan's, 68; of false, 137; of mixtures, 44 et seq.; of three, 11 et seq., 40 et seq.

Science, history of, 22; development of, vii et seq.
Seven, tests of divisibility by, 35.
Short-mind symbols, vii et seq.
Signs + and —, 57.
Squaring of the circle, 62.
Stenophrenic symbols, vii et seq.
Straight line, 144.
Substitutions, 111 et seq., 123.
Subtraction, new method of, 25 et seq.
Sum and difference, of two numbers, 56.
Supposition, rule of, 137, 148.
Symbols, vii et seq.

Tables, 137; expedient for supplying lacunæ in, 148.
Tannery, M. Paul, 58 footnote, 151.
Tartaglia, 60, 61.
Temperament, theory of, 23.
Theon, 59.
Theory and practice, 43.

Theory of remainders, utility of the, 38.
Third degree, equations of the, 71, 82.
Three roots, reality of the, 93.
Trial and error, rule of, 137, 148.
Trisection of an angle, 62, 81.
Turks, 58.

Undetermined quantities, 82.
Unity, three cubic roots of, 72.
Unknown quantity, 55.

Values, mean, 45 et seq.; minimal, 132.
Variations, calculus of, x.
Vatican library, 58.
Vieta, viii, 62, 65.
Vlacq, 20.

Wallis, viii.
Wertheim, G.. 58 footnote.
Woodhouse, x.

Xylander, 58.

CATALOGUE OF PUBLICATIONS

OF THE

OPEN COURT PUBLISHING CO.

COPE, E. D.
THE PRIMARY FACTORS OF ORGANIC EVOLUTION.
121 cuts. Pp. xvi, 547. Cloth, $2.00 (10s.).

MÜLLER, F. MAX.
THREE INTRODUCTORY LECTURES ON THE SCIENCE OF THOUGHT.
128 pages. Cloth, 75c (3s. 6d.).

THREE LECTURES ON THE SCIENCE OF LANGUAGE.
112 pages. 2nd Edition. Cloth, 75c (3s. 6d.).

ROMANES, GEORGE JOHN.
DARWIN AND AFTER DARWIN.
Three Vols., $4.00. Singly, as follows:
1. THE DARWINIAN THEORY. 460 pages. 125 illustrations. Cloth, $2.00
2. POST-DARWINIAN QUESTIONS. Heredity and Utility. Pp. 338. $1.50
3. POST-DARWINIAN QUESTIONS. Isolation and Physiological Selection Pp. 181. $1.00.

AN EXAMINATION OF WEISMANNISM.
236 pages. Cloth, $1.00.

THOUGHTS ON RELIGION.
Third Edition, Pages, 184. Cloth, gilt top, $1.25.

SHUTE, DR. D. KERFOOT.
FIRST BOOK IN ORGANIC EVOLUTION.
9 colored plates, 39 cuts. Pp. xvi + 285. Price, $2.00 (7s. 6d.).

MACH, ERNST.
THE SCIENCE OF MECHANICS.
Translated by T. J. McCormack. 250 cuts. 534 pages. $2.50 (12s. 6d.)

POPULAR SCIENTIFIC LECTURES.
Third Edition. 415 pages. 59 cuts. Cloth, gilt top. $1.50 (7s. 6d.).

THE ANALYSIS OF THE SENSATIONS.
Pp. 208. 37 cuts. Cloth, $1.25 (6s. 6d.).

LAGRANGE, JOSEPH LOUIS.
LECTURES ON ELEMENTARY MATHEMATICS.
With portrait of the author. Pp. 172. Price, $1.00 (5s.).

DE MORGAN, AUGUSTUS.
ON THE STUDY AND DIFFICULTIES OF MATHEMATICS.
New Reprint edition with notes. Pp. viii + 288. Cloth, $1.25 (5s.).

ELEMENTARY ILLUSTRATIONS OF THE DIFFERENTIAL AND INTEGRAL CALCULUS.
New reprint edition. Price, $1.00 (5s.).

FINK, KARL.
A BRIEF HISTORY OF MATHEMATICS.
Trans. by W. W. Beman and D. E. Smith. Pp., 333. Cloth, $1.50 (5s.6d.)

SCHUBERT, HERMANN.
MATHEMATICAL ESSAYS AND RECREATIONS.
Pp. 149. Cuts, 37. Cloth, 75c (3s. 6d.).

HUC AND GABET, MM.
TRAVELS IN TARTARY, THIBET AND CHINA.
100 engravings. Pp 28 + 660. 2 vols. $2.00 (10s.). One vol., $1.25 (5s.)

CARUS, PAUL.
THE HISTORY OF THE DEVIL, AND THE IDEA OF EVIL.
311 Illustrations. Pages, 500. Price, $6.00 (30s.).
EROS AND PSYCHE.
Retold after Apuleius. With Illustrations by Paul Thumann. Pp. 125. Price, $1.50 (6s.).
WHENCE AND WHITHER?
An Inquiry into the Nature of the Soul. 196 pages. Cloth, 75c (3s. 6d.)
THE ETHICAL PROBLEM.
Second edition, revised and enlarged. 351 pages. Cloth, $1.25 (6s. 6d.)
FUNDAMENTAL PROBLEMS.
Second edition, revised and enlarged. 372 pp. Cl., $1.50 (7s. 6d.).
HOMILIES OF SCIENCE.
317 pages. Cloth, Gilt Top, $1.50 (7s. 6d.).
THE IDEA OF GOD.
Fourth edition. 32 pages. Paper, 15c (9d.).
THE SOUL OF MAN.
2nd ed. 182 cuts. 482 pages. Cloth, $1.50 (6s.).
TRUTH IN FICTION. TWELVE TALES WITH A MORAL.
White and gold binding, gilt edges. Pp. 111. $1.00 (5s.).
THE RELIGION OF SCIENCE.
Second, extra edition. Pp. 103. Price, 50c (2s. 6d.).
PRIMER OF PHILOSOPHY.
240 pages. Second Edition. Cloth, $1.00 (5s.).
THE GOSPEL OF BUDDHA. According to Old Records.
Fifth Edition. Pp. 275. Cloth, $1.00 (5s.). In German, $1.25 (6s. 6d.)
BUDDHISM AND ITS CHRISTIAN CRITICS.
Pages, 311. Cloth, $1.25 (6s. 6d.).
KARMA. A STORY OF EARLY BUDDHISM.
Illustrated by Japanese artists. Crêpe paper, 75c (3s. 6d.).
NIRVANA: A STORY OF BUDDHIST PSYCHOLOGY.
Japanese edition, like *Karma*. $1.00 (4s. 6d.).
LAO-TZE'S TAO-TEH-KING.
Chinese-English. Pp. 360. Cloth, $3.00 (15s.).

CORNILL, CARL HEINRICH.
THE PROPHETS OF ISRAEL.
Pp., 200 Cloth, $1.00 (5s.).
HISTORY OF THE PEOPLE OF ISRAEL.
Pp. vi + 325. Cloth, $1.50 (7s. 6d.).

POWELL, J. W.
TRUTH AND ERROR; or, the Science of Intellection.
Pp. 423. Cloth, $1.75 (7s. 6d.).

RIBOT, TH.
THE PSYCHOLOGY OF ATTENTION.
THE DISEASES OF PERSONALITY.
THE DISEASES OF THE WILL.
Cloth, 75 cents each (3s. 6d.). *Full set, cloth, $1.75* (9s.).
EVOLUTION OF GENERAL IDEAS.
Pp. 231. Cloth, $1.25 (5s.).

WAGNER, RICHARD.
A PILGRIMAGE TO BEETHOVEN.
A Story. With portrait of Beethoven. Pp. 40. Boards, 50c (2s. 6d.).

HUTCHINSON, WOODS.
THE GOSPEL ACCORDING TO DARWIN.
Pp. xii + 241. Price, $1.50 (6s.).

FREYTAG, GUSTAV.
THE LOST MANUSCRIPT. A Novel.
2 vols. 953 pages. Extra cloth, $4.00 (21s.). One vol., cl., $1.00 (5s.)
MARTIN LUTHER.
Illustrated. Pp. 130. Cloth, $1.00 (5s.).

AÇVAGHOSHA.
: DISCOURSE ON THE AWAKENING OF FAITH in the Mahâyâna.
Translated for the first time from the Chinese version by Tietaro
Suzuki. Pages, 176. Price, cloth, $1.25 (5s. 6d.).

TRUMBULL, M. M.
: THE FREE TRADE STRUGGLE IN ENGLAND.
Second Edition. 296 pages. Cloth, 75c (3s. 6d.).
: WHEELBARROW: ARTICLES AND DISCUSSIONS ON THE LABOR QUESTION.
With portrait of the author. 303 pages. Cloth, $1.00 (5s.).

GOETHE AND SCHILLER'S XENIONS.
: Translated by Paul Carus. Album form. Pp. 162. Cl., $1.00 (5s.).

OLDENBERG, H.
: ANCIENT INDIA: ITS LANGUAGE AND RELIGIONS.
Pp. 100. Cloth, 50c (2s. 6d.).

CONWAY, DR. MONCURE DANIEL.
: SOLOMON, AND SOLOMONIC LITERATURE.
Pp. 243. Cloth, $1.50 (6s.).

GARBE, RICHARD.
: THE REDEMPTION OF THE BRAHMAN. A TALE OF HINDU LIFE.
Laid paper. Gilt top. 96 pages. Price, 75c (3s. 6d.).
: THE PHILOSOPHY OF ANCIENT INDIA.
Pp. 89. Cloth, 50c (2s. 6d.).

HUEPPE, FERDINAND.
: THE PRINCIPLES OF BACTERIOLOGY.
28 Woodcuts. Pp. x + 467. Price, $1.75 (9s.).

LÉVY-BRUHL, PROF. L.
: HISTORY OF MODERN PHILOSOPHY IN FRANCE.
23 Portraits. Handsomely bound. Pp. 500. Price, $3.00 (12s.).

TOPINARD, DR. PAUL.
: SCIENCE AND FAITH, OR MAN AS AN ANIMAL AND MAN AS A MEMBER OF SOCIETY.
Pp. 374. Cloth, $1.50 (6s. 6d.).

BINET, ALFRED.
: THE PSYCHOLOGY OF REASONING.
Pp. 193. Cloth, 75c (3s. 6d.).
: THE PSYCHIC LIFE OF MICRO-ORGANISMS.
Pp. 135. Cloth, 75 cents.
: ON DOUBLE CONSCIOUSNESS.
See No. 8, Religion of Science Library.

THE OPEN COURT.
: A Monthly Magazine Devoted to the Science of Religion, the Religion of Science, and the Extension of the Religious Parliament Idea.
Terms: $1.00 a year; 5s. 6d. to foreign countries in the Postal Union. Single Copies, 10 cents (6d.).

THE MONIST.
: A Quarterly Magazine of Philosophy and Science.
Per copy, 50 cents; Yearly, $2.00. In England and all countries in U.P.U. per copy, 2s. 6d.: Yearly, 9s. 6d.

CHICAGO:

THE OPEN COURT PUBLISHING CO.
Monon Building, 324 Dearborn St.

LONDON: Kegan Paul, Trench, Trübner & Company, Ltd.

The Religion of Science Library.

A collection of bi-monthly publications, most of which are reprints of books published by The Open Court Publishing Company. Yearly, $1.50. Separate copies according to prices quoted. The books are printed upon good paper, from large type.
The Religion of Science Library, by its extraordinarily reasonable price will place a large number of valuable books within the reach of all readers. The following have already appeared in the series:

No. 1. *The Religion of Science.* By PAUL CARUS. 25c (1s. 6d.).
  2. *Three Introductory Lectures on the Science of Thought.* By F. MAX MÜLLER. 25c (1s. 6d.).
  3. *Three Lectures on the Science of Language.* F. MAX MÜLLER. 25c (1s.6d.)
  4. *The Diseases of Personality.* By TH. RIBOT. 25c (1s. 6d.).
  5. *The Psychology of Attention.* By TH. RIBOT. 25c (1s. 6d.).
  6. *The Psychic Life of Micro-Organisms.* By ALFRED BINET. 25c (1s. 6d.)
  7. *The Nature of the State.* By PAUL CARUS. 15c (9d.).
  8. *On Double Consciousness.* By ALFRED BINET. 15c (9d.).
  9. *Fundamental Problems.* By PAUL CARUS. 50c (2s. 6d.).
  10. *The Diseases of the Will.* By TH. RIBOT. 25c (1s. 6d.).
  11. *The Origin of Language.* By LUDWIG NOIRE. 15c (9d.).
  12. *The Free Trade Struggle in England.* M. M. TRUMBULL. 25c (1s. 6d.)
  13. *Wheelbarrow on the Labor Question.* By M. M. TRUMBULL. 35c (2s.).
  14. *The Gospel of Buddha.* By PAUL CARUS. 35c (2s.).
  15. *The Primer of Philosophy.* By PAUL CARUS. 25c (1s. 6d.).
  16. *On Memory,* and *The Specific Energies of the Nervous System.* By PROF. EWALD HERING. 15c (9d.).
  17. *The Redemption of the Brahman.* Tale of Hindu Life. By RICHARD GARBE. 25c (1s. 6d.).
  18. *An Examination of Weismannism.* By G. J. ROMANES. 35c (2s.).
  19. *On Germinal Selection.* By AUGUST WEISMANN. 25c (1s. 6d.).
  20. *Lovers Three Thousand Years Ago.* By T. A. GOODWIN. (Out of print.)
  21. *Popular Scientific Lectures.* By ERNST MACH. 50c (2s. 6d.).
  22. *Ancient India: Its Language and Religions.* By H. OLDENBERG. 25c (1s. 6d.).
  23. *The Prophets of Israel.* By PROF. C. H. CORNILL. 25c (1. 6d.).
  24. *Homilies of Science.* By PAUL CARUS. 35c (2s.).
  25. *Thoughts on Religion.* By G. J. ROMANES. 50c (2s. 6d.).
  26. *The Philosophy of Ancient India.* By PROF. RICHARD GARBE. 25c (1s. 6d.)
  27. *Martin Luther.* By GUSTAV FREYTAG. 25c (1s. 6d.).
  28. *English Secularism.* By GEORGE JACOB HOLYOAKE. 25c (1s. 6d.).
  29. *On Orthogenesis.* By TH. EIMER. 25c (1s. 6d.).
  30. *Chinese Philosophy.* By PAUL CARUS. 25c (1s. 6d.).
  31. *The Lost Manuscript.* By GUSTAV FREYTAG. 60c (3s.).
  32. *A Mechanico-Physiological Theory of Organic Evolution.* By CARL VON NAEGELI. 15c (9d.).
  33. *Chinese Fiction.* By DR. GEORGE T. CANDLIN. 15c (9d.).
  34. *Mathematical Essays and Recreations.* By H. SCHUBERT. 25c (1s. 6d.)
  35. *The Ethical Problem.* By PAUL CARUS. 50c (2s. 6d.).
  36. *Buddhism and Its Christian Critics.* By PAUL CARUS. 50c (2s. 6d.).
  37. *Psychology for Beginners.* By HIRAM M. STANLEY. 20c (1s.).
  38. *Discourse on Method.* By DESCARTES. 25c (1s. 6d.).
  39. *The Dawn of a New Era.* By PAUL CARUS. 15c (9d.).
  40. *Kant and Spencer.* By PAUL CARUS. 20c (1s.).
  41. *The Soul of Man.* By PAUL CARUS. 75c (3s. 6d.).
  42. *World's Congress Addresses.* By C. C. BONNEY. 15c (9d.).
  43. *The Gospel According to Darwin.* By WOODS HUTCHINSON. 50c (2s. 6d.)
  44. *Whence and Whither.* By PAUL CARUS. 25c (1s.6d.).
  45. *Enquiry Concerning Human Understanding.* By DAVID HUME. 25c (1s. 6d.).
  46. *Enquiry Concerning the Principles of Morals.* By DAVID HUME. 25c (1s. 6d.).

THE OPEN COURT PUBLISHING CO.,
CHICAGO : 324 DEARBORN STREET.
LONDON: Kegan Paul, Trench, Trübner & Company, Ltd.

www.ingramcontent.com/pod-product-compliance
Lightning Source LLC
Chambersburg PA
CBHW031447160426
43195CB00010BB/891